mouth Street Baths was a cindered open space known as Grange Street Croft and on the left of the croft stood the Backward School, known to us children as the "Dunces' School". The site on the right of the croft was occupied by the new red brick building, Grange Street Senior School, with playgrounds front and rear. During the 1914-1918 War this building was used as a military hospital.

From our shop in Wellington Street, looking in the direction of Grey Mare Lane, only two hundred yards away was the prominent winding gear of Bradford Pit. This was a useful landmark when returning from my wanderings around the district. I soon discovered the "Little Park" between Barmouth Street and Gresham Street (now Charlesworth Street). There was a red shale playground with swings, a bowling green at one end and a bandstand in the centre, all well used and appreciated. At the opposite end was Johnson Street School, opened in August 1891 and blackened by 25 years of industrial and domestic soot and grime. The "Little Park" was the school playground.

The things I remember most about my short time at Grange Street Infants' School are learning to lace up my shoes, modelling with clay, Bible stories and running errands for teachers' dinners. They knew I lived in a shop, so about ten minutes before twelve o'clock they would send me home to bring them such things as four barm cakes, two pennyworth of corned beef, three pennyworth of boiled ham, two pennyworth of cheese and four pennyworth of "nice" currant cake. The War was on, and they got these things "off the ration"; this, I was a mistake; I had no interest or aptitude at the age of six. I had only recently started school and could not write properly, sometimes writing letters back to front, even upside down, so I was definitely not ready. I don't think I progressed beyond five finger exercises. "Madam Jeffreys" used to sit me at the piano and say, "Play that five finger exercise and I'll be back in a few minutes". The next thing I would hear was her scrubbing the floor upstairs or washing pots in the kitchen, so I don't think failure was all my fault. The happiest thing I remember during my brief spell with Mrs Jeffreys was the occasion when I took part in a concert, along with her other pupils, to entertain the wounded soldiers at the requisitioned Grange Street School.

The grief and sorrow of the war was a fact of life with which I grew up. It was a common sight to see women in their shawls crying in our shop, between sobs saying, "Our Tom", "Dick" or "Harry" "is missing on the Somme", or "Passchendaele". On the other hand, a woman might say, "We've had good news; our George hasn't been killed – we've been informed he's a prisoner of war." An everyday sight was soldiers in hospital blue, bandaged, on crutches or occasionally being wheeled in a cane wheelchair.

There was an abundance of local characters, such as Blind Billy, who used to walk the

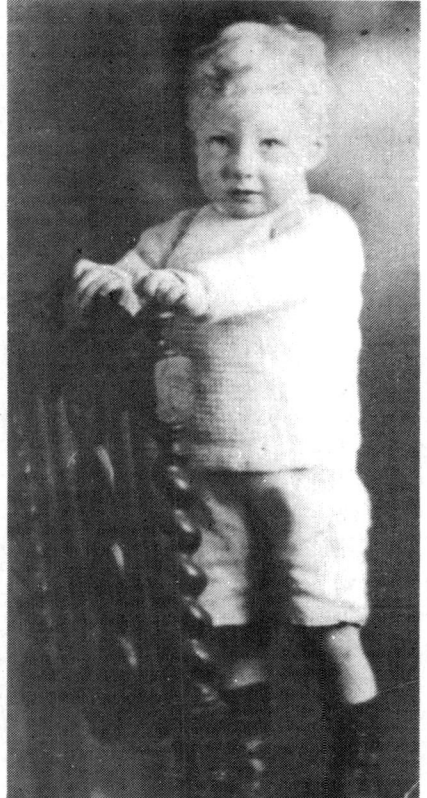

The author aged 2

streets delivering morning and evening newspapers. In addition to being totally blind, he had the handicap of a "peg leg". I understand his injuries had been inflicted during the Boer War. Nevertheless, he was a lively, cheerful soul who went about his business with remarkable gusto. The noise made by his "peg leg" on the flagstones, his stick striking the walls or doors and his whistling of the popular tunes of the day heralded his coming hundreds of yards away. How he knew which houses and shops to deliver the newspapers to puzzled my young mind, and still intrigues me even today.

Knocker Charlie, the knocker-up, was a chap who was mostly heard but rarely seen. Sometimes I was awakened between four and five o'clock in the morning as he rattled his rods on nearby windows, rousing workers for the early morning shifts. Soon afterwards, the clatter of clogs could be heard as the miners and mill girls made their way to Bradford Pit, and to the cotton mills in Bradford and Ancoats.

Another well known character was Mokey Taylor, the flitting man. He was a very small, bow-legged chap who always wore a bowler hat. The words "Moses Taylor, Removals" were painted on the sides of his large horse-drawn vans, but people knew him as Mokey, the man who would do a flitting for them at a reasonable price.

Changing shift at Bradford Pit, 1911

Dr Hargreaves, a well-liked man who had his surgery at the corner of Cross Street and Grey Mare Lane, was a particular favourite of mine. In 1916 my mother, who had to run the business and look after two small boys single-handed, became very run down in health. Dr Hargreaves prescribed that Mother should drink a Guinness each day, so she bought a dozen bottles each week from McCabe's outdoor beer licence, one of the shops in our row at that time. I don't know whether this was a crafty ploy by the good doctor, or merely a coincidence, but he continued to check Mother's progress about twice a week for several months. Visits were always during the afternoon, after he had done his round and before his evening surgery. I can visualize him now, coming through our shop and into the living room, to be handed a bottle of Guinness and a glass. He would sit down at our new piano and entertain himself for a couple of hours. Meanwhile, between attending to customers, Mother would chat to him and listen to his delightful playing.

Opposite Dr Hargreaves' surgery on Grey Mare Lane was Heywood's hay and corn shop, where the many horse owners purchased their horses' feed. Many people kept hens in their backyards or on the allotments off Seymour Road, Clayton, which enabled them to supplement their wartime rations. The corner between Cross Street and Wellington Street was occupied by Moss's pawnshop. On Monday mornings one could see women in shawls with bundles wrapped in paper clutched to their bosoms, waiting for "Uncle" to open his shop. Then on Friday nights, after wages had been paid, they would be back to redeem their pledges so that husbands, sons or daughters could wear their "Sunday best" at the pictures or theatre on Saturday night, or at church on Sunday.

After the Armistice

I remember Armistice Day, 1918, as plainly as yesterday. It must have been anticipated, because we were sent home from school for the rest of the day. Late in the morning, I was playing football with the boys in our back entry. The girls were playing hop scotch in the square at the rear of Mokey Taylor's yard, when suddenly the women started coming out of their houses with shouts of joy, some laughing and some crying in relief. Bells rang, heralding the glad news, and newspaper sellers shouted, "Special! War ended!" Groups of people chatted excitedly on the street and the atmosphere vibrated with the gleeful noises of rejoicing. Children entered into the spirit of that happy day by collecting any old rubbish to light bonfires. Wellington Street, Nelson Street and Cross Street were quickly decorated with flags hanging from the upstairs windows, and bunting hung across the streets. Among all the Union Jacks on our street, the Belgian flag of a family who had fled their country on the outbreak of war waved proudly to signal their joy. That special night I was allowed to stay up extra late before I was called in from the bonfire with smoke-blackened face and dirty hands; very tired, but extremely happy and contented.

Between Armistice Day, November 11th 1918, and Peace Day, June 28th 1919, most of the school singing sessions were confined to learning patriotic songs. Other school songs, such as "Early One Morning", "Golden Slumbers", "Come to the Fair" and "Where the Bee Sucks" (the second line of which, according to the boys on the back row, was, "In a cow flop dell I lie") were shelved for "Land of Hope and Glory", "Land of Our Fathers", "The Minstrel Boy", "Auld Lang Syne" and "The Marseillaise".

Peace Day was spent keeping the bonfire blazing, roasting spuds, playing games, eating jelly and custard, drinking pop and singing the songs we had learnt at school. At eight o'clock, my parents, having shut the shop, called me in and packed me off to bed. On the table in front of the bedroom window my mother had placed a large plate of lettuce, radishes, fresh bread and butter and a bowl of apples and toffees. "You can eat that lot and look through the window until it starts to go dark," she said. Dad and Mother then went to the club to enjoy the peace celebrations for a couple of hours. It was midsummer, light until almost eleven o'clock, so I concentrated on devouring the feast before looking through the window. There was plenty going on down our street; revellers shouting, singing and waving flags as they made their way to the pubs and clubs. As darkness fell, the drunks, and the sober, of course, began to tumble out of the Vic, some collecting their children who had been left round the doorway. Some men had children racing for pennies, running as far as the "bogy hole" where men played "pitch and toss" on Sundays, then back to the Vic. Tiredness gradually got the better of me, so I tumbled into bed. Soon I was slumbering so deeply that I did not hear my parents come home, to awake next morning with memories which would last me all my life.

Dyemaking at Clayton Aniline, 1934

In 1919 the war-wounded had left the new school in Grange Street and it reverted to the purpose for which it had been built. So I was transferred from Johnson Street (where I had attended "half time" after reaching Standard 2 at Grange Street) to Standard 3 at Grange Street. My teacher was a Miss Baguley, a dark-haired lady who wore gold-rimmed spectacles, and the headmaster was a grey-haired man called Mr Ashton. I thought the new school was marvellous after my three years in the old Infants' School and Johnson Street.

On Saturday mornings I enjoyed watching the school football team play their matches on the Donkey Common, a red shale recreation ground bounded on two sides by the backyards and gable ends of small terraced houses. On the other sides were Birley Street Elementary School and the railway with its footbridge leading into Viaduct Street. Several schools used the Donkey Common as their home ground, it being the only suitable public ground in the district. Both Grange Street and Johnson Street had very good football teams in those days. One lad in particular at Grange Street was Fitton, who played for Manchester Boys and later for West Bromwich Albion for a number of seasons.

Once I went as far as the Manchester City ground at Hyde Road to see Manchester Boys play South Shields Boys. One boy on view that day was Cresswell, who in the 1920s became one of England's best-ever full backs. The first professional football match, late in the war years, was at the old Hyde Road ground, which was actually in Bennett Street. I went on my own, and I can recall my walk along Grey Mare Lane, Pottery Lane, round by Ashburys Station, into Gorton Road, past Vaughan's Crane Works and into Bennett Street, to arrive at the ground in an excited mood. City was playing Chelsea; the City wingers were Spud Murphy and the legendary Welsh international, Billy Meredith.

Around that time, there was an amateur team called Bradford United, who played their home matches on Mill Street Croft, facing the Police Station. They attracted crowds for their home games that many of today's professional teams would be delighted with. After the War, my dad played for a team from the club in Grey Mare Lane, Bradford Junior Unionist. He used to take me to watch him play and this took me to Gorton, Openshaw, Collyhurst, Cheetham, and to what to me were far away places with strange sounding names - Ladybarn, Northenden and Chorlton-cum-Hardy. I was probably more interested in the tramcar travel than the football and I must have learned quite a lot about Manchester that way.

In the War years, even up to 1921, a motor car, van or lorry was a rare sight. Most goods were transported by horse-drawn carts, and there was a fair number of steam-powered wagons chugging along the streets, with their glowing red fires, pumping clouds of smoke from their chimneys. Leggott's of Clayton, near to the Belsize motor car works, had a small fleet of these vehicles. During the Great War, Belsize was busy on war work, but went out of business soon afterwards. The first taxi-cab I saw was a Belsize. However, the horse continued to be the main motive power for local deliveries well into the 1920s. Billy Benson, the greengrocer at the corner of Wellington Street and Albert Street, could be seen about three times a week making his way with his horse and cart to Smithfield Market. Mr Applewhite, the butcher in our row, had a pony and trap for collecting his meat and also used it for pleasure, especially on Monday afternoons (butchers' half-day closing) when many of them gathered at the Audenshaw Trotting Track at the rear of the Snipe Hotel. The railway companies made their local deliveries by horse and lorry from the Ancoats, Deansgate, Oldham Road and Liverpool Road Goods Depots.

Some of my childhood landmarks are best remembered, not for their architectural design or natural beauty, but for the appetising smells or obnoxious odours issuing from them. Who could ever forget the smell of bread and cakes being baked at Bradshaw's cake shop, or the aroma of spring flowers or fresh summer fruits and vegetables coming from Billy Benson's shop on the corner of Albert Street? There was the smell of meat being cut up at Applewhite's butchers, not forgetting the lovely smell of potato pie and cooked meats wafting from our shop in Wellington Street.

As for the stinks, there was the reek of stale beer and smoke from the Victoria Inn at the junction of Wellington Street and Grey Mare Lane. Here the boys played a game of dare, running through the Wellington Street entrance, past the drinkers at the bar and out of the Grey Mare Lane door. Then there was the terrific "buzz" of horse dung from Billy Benson's stable, and the foul odour, especially in hot weather, from the men's urinal adjacent to the stables. But far worse was the horrible stench of tripe boiling and dressing which pervaded the district, coming from Pendlebury's Tripe Works at the side of Grey Mare Lane Market. A short walk up Ashton New Road towards Clayton on certain days of the week, and one could find oneself gasping for breath. The fumes from the Clayton Aniline factory caused smarting eyes, and combined with the rank smell from the nearby Dean & Wood's knacker yard in Gibbon Street to make the walk to Clayton Park or the Dingle an unpleasant experience at times.

The 53 tram, photographed in 1930

All Kinds of Entertainment

Places of entertainment featured prominently in my childhood. The first theatre I visited was the Manchester Hippodrome on Oxford Street. I remember walking down a gaslit Portland Street holding my dad's hand, and as we walked he was briefing me as to what I had to reply if my mother asked me which school I wanted to go to. Suddenly, to my relief, the bright lights of the "Hip" drew my attention and I was able to divert the conversation. Once inside the theatre, my eyes were all over the place. It was a lovely theatre, with a circle in front of the stalls used for circus performances, or it could be flooded for an aqua-show. When the theatre was closed to make way for the Gaumont Cinema I thought it was such a shame; to me it was the best theatre in Manchester.

The Metropole on Ashton Old Road, one of the Broadhead's circuit, was a favourite of mine, probably because it was the nearest theatre to my home. In the pantomime season my dad would give me twopence (admittance to the gallery) to get rid of me for a couple of hours on a Saturday afternoon. It used to be hilarious. The noise at times was deafening; what with the booing of the demon king, the wicked uncle, the giant or the ugly sisters, and the cheering of the principal boy, Jolly Jack the sailor, Buttons or the entry of the good fairy, there was never a dull moment. There would be battles fought with orange peel and much bawling and shouting to friend or foe in other parts of the theatre. The seating in the gallery was a series of bare wooden stairs, rising almost to the roof. Many a time boys at the top would have a "Jimmy Riddle" and see whose stream could descend the most steps. It must have been an ordeal performing to that lot!

My first picture show was a magic lantern lecture at Bradford Memorial School at the corner of Cross Street and Howarth Street. This school always fascinated me, with its playground on the flat roof where the children could be seen standing at the railings, shouting down to people in the street below. The school was attached to St Cuthbert's Church, and the lantern lectures, mainly of a biblical nature, consisted of still pictures flashed on to a white sheet hung against a wall.

Far more interesting were the silent movies at the New Royal Picture House on Ashton New Road, next to the District Nurses' Home. The New Royal was one of the many picture palaces built early this century. There was a Mosley Cinema in Stott Street, at the rear of the Mosley Hotel on Ashton New Road, and about 1920 there was a picture house on Ashton New Road, on the opposite corner to the Manchester Slate Company; but this soon closed to reopen as a billiard hall. On Grey Mare Lane, facing Proctor's the vet, where I remember taking dogs to be put down, stood the Prince's Picture House. After the Saturday afternoon "penny crush" let out, the adjoining small fairground was patronised by many of the children.

At the age of seven or eight I was interested in music and dancing. It was a frequent topic of conversation with my parents and their friends from the Bradford Junior Unionist Club. There was the one night a week when Mother left Dad to look after the shop and my brother and I, to go dancing at Ashton Palais de Danse. Off she would go with Ada Moss from the pawnshop and Ethel Hill, a war widow from Grey Mare Lane. Ashton Palais was extremely popular in those days; it had a fine big ballroom floor, and the Will Hurst Dance Orchestra was reckoned to be the best for miles around. In the early 1920s, the band went to the beautiful Palace Ballroom, Blackpool, where they remained as resident orchestra for many years.

Two popular dance halls in our area were Rowsley Street Co-op Hall and New Islington Hall, near to New Islington Baths, one of Manchester's first swimming baths. I have fond memories of both halls on the occasions when my father and his friends held Saturday night dances there. He took me along with him several times and sat me at the side of the stage, where I could watch the dancing and listen to the orchestra. One of the bands was the Garner Schofield Orchestra, regarded as the best (non-resident) gig band in the Manchester area. They could be heard on 2ZY Manchester in the early days of the wireless.

The streets of Bradford consisted mainly of rows of two up, two down houses with outside lavatories. Nelson Street, Parker Street, Cross Street, Howarth Street, Butterworth Street, Mill Street, Birch Street, Chatham Street, Lime Street and Barlow Street, to name but a few, were typical of the district. A few of the slightly larger houses on Wellington Street and Grey Mare Lane had cellars, where the family wash could be done, or coal stored. Families lived in cramped conditions; small rooms and bedrooms with little furniture. Although our family was only four at the shop in Wellington Street, we had little privacy. We could escape to the lavatory in the backyard, but even then

Oxford Street and the Manchester Hippodrome

it would not be long before someone would shout, "How long are you going to sit out there? I'm waiting to come on there!" Which reminds me of a dark winter's night when I was sitting peacefully on the throne and I heard a rhythmic bumping noise coming from the backyard door. Fastening up my trousers, I tiptoed to the back door and gently slid back the bolt. To my amazement, into the yard, in a heap, fell a courting couple. I retreated quickly into the house to tell my mother, but she only laughed. Years later, I realised the significance of what I had done.

I was about seven years old when I made my first trip to what was then known as Higher Openshaw. One sunny Saturday morning I went with my playmate Arthur Millard, from the toffee shop next door but one, to the Pack Horse Hotel to pay his father's union dues. We walked there and back, passing the great Armstrong Whitworth Works, Whitworth Hall and Baths. The name Whitworth could be heard many times a day in Openshaw, Bradford, Clayton and Gorton, where most of Armstrong Whitworth's employees lived.

On Ashton Old Road, near Whitworth Hall, Crossley Lads' Club was one of Manchester's best known institutions. Their sports ground was on the site now occupied by St Willibrord's Church, North Road, Clayton.

Engineering was the predominant industry in Openshaw and Gorton, employing thousands of local workers, many of them at the Gorton Locomotive Works (Gorton Tank to the locals) down Cornwall Street. The site is now occupied by the new Smithfield Market. They had a canteen and a good club in Cornwall Street, where some years later I played for dancing on several occasions. Between the two Great Wars, one couldn't go wrong for dance halls along Ashton Old Road. In Higher Openshaw, between Old Lane and Fairfield Road, was the Alhambra Dance Hall, better known as Chick Hibbert's, a very popular place with dancing six nights a week. At the other end of the road, in Lower Openshaw above the Beswick Co-op, was Walsh's. Later it became Billy Hall's, under what to me was a most peculiar name for a dance hall, the Lido. I always imagined a lido as a swimming bath or a pleasure beach with a swimming pool. On the corner of Grey Mare Lane, over Burton's the Tailors, was the Burton Ballroom, and close by the great Armstrong Whitworth works was the Granville Dance Hall, above the Openshaw Liberal Club.

Family Matters

Openshaw, Bradford, and Gorton, second only to Trafford Park in importance as an industrial centre, was not a healthy place to live. The big difference between there and Trafford Park was the density of the population; there were very few houses in Trafford Park, whereas in East Manchester thousands of small terraced houses were packed between the great engineering factories. The air was filthy, always with a smell of smoke from the thousands of factory and house chimneys, so that when people blew their noses half a dozen times their handkerchiefs were blackened with soot. Bronchial troubles of all kinds were common and tuberculosis - most people called it consumption in those days - was a prevalent disease in Manchester when I was young; except in relation to cattle, the word is rarely heard today.

My maternal grandparents lived at 323 Mill Street, facing Birch Street and St Brigid's Church. Grandfather O'Conner was a candlemaker who worked for Price's, the famous candlemakers of London, before bringing his family to Manchester about 1893. Before the Great War he worked at the CWS Candle Factory, Irlam, which at a later date turned to the production of margarine. After the outbreak of war, he worked on munitions at the big Armstrong-Whitworth works in Openshaw. He was on shift work at the furnaces, and sweated profusely. At the end of the shift he would make his way home in the cold night, or early morning, air. Eventually he contracted tuberculosis, which landed him in Baguley Sanatorium for "open air" treatment.

Another childhood experience I will never forget was a visit to Baguley with my mother on a bitterly cold day. We boarded the "bogie tram" (No. 53 single decker) which took us on the "circular route" as far as the Birch Villa Hotel. Then on to a double decker, along Wilmslow Road, passing Platt Fields, to the West Didsbury terminus. From there I had the thrill of riding on my first motor-bus. Until then I hadn't known that such a vehicle existed and like most little boys I wanted to go on the open upper deck, but Mother dragged me inside, much to my disappointment. Through the roads of posh houses and gardens of Didsbury, into the leafy lanes of Cheshire, the bus made its way to the hospital. Baguley Sanatorium was then surrounded by good farmland. We found Grandfather in a bed on an open verandah, with a biting wind blowing directly on to it. On our return home, I remember Mother telling Dad

Armstrong Whitworth's in 1922. Running 60 tons of molten steel into a ladle

that if Grandfather didn't come out of that place quickly, he would be dead in a week or so. Within days he was back home, and though suffering gradually worsening health, he lasted another eight years.

Most of Mother's relatives lived close by St Brigid's Church, in Mill Street, Birch Street and Lime Street. Her eldest sister was married to John Hughes, a coal miner at Bradford Pit. Uncle John kept pigeons in their backyard in Birch Street and whenever he came home from the pit he first went to look at his pigeons. Aunt Polly got fed up with putting Uncle John's dinner on the table to go cold while he was out admiring his birds and she used to say, "He thinks more about those bloody birds than he does about me." One day, in came Uncle John, straight into the backyard, as usual. No sooner through the back door than he was back shouting, "Where's my pigeons?" Taking a large basin from the oven and putting it in front of him, Aunt Polly bawled, "There's your bloody pigeons, and I hope they choke you!" Aunt Polly was certainly a rum card. She worked at the mill and left home at 5.30am, sometimes leaving Uncle John in bed when he was on afternoon shift. He had a reputation for laziness and sometimes, when Aunt Polly came home for lunch, he would still be in bed. One day, on finding him slumbering, oblivious to the fact that he should be getting himself ready for work, she took the nearly-full "jerry" from under the bed and poured the contents all over him, giving him a really good awakening. I don't know what transpired then, but I do know they remained married until Aunt Polly died through a fall from a ladder while cleaning windows.

Mother had inherited the same kind of spirit. Wright & Green Ltd, Wholesale Grocers, Hanging Ditch, supplied our shop with most groceries from a horse-drawn cart, but we had bread delivered from two separate bakeries, both by horse-drawn bread vans. (I loved to feed the horses with stale bread.) Tip Top was one firm, and Holland's of Openshaw the other. A Mr Chapman was Holland's bread man, and I witnessed several of Mother's battles with him when he tried to palm her off with stale bread. He would carry the bread into the shop on a large wooden tray, and with some convivial patter try to put Mother off her guard. But Mother was a hard nut to crack. She would test every loaf for freshness and on finding a stale one, would sling it back across the counter at poor Mr Chapman, remarking emphatically, "You can take that back for a start." I think Mr Chapman dreaded coming to our shop.

My early memories of Dad are nearly all connected with trips to football matches. Manchester United moved from the Bank Street, Clayton, ground to their new ground at Old Trafford in 1910 and one of the highlights of my childhood was when he took me to the new ground to watch a game between United and West Bromwich Albion. The player I most remember was Jesse Pennington, the famous Albion and England international full back.

My dad used to tell me about a printing error in the Football Chronicle concerning the pre-war United side. The report on a certain game said, "Meredith centred the ball to Turnbull, who shit wildly over the bar." There were stories I overheard about Tommy Browell, the post-war centre forward of Manchester City. Tommy was well known for his trick of "heading goals with his hand". He would position himself on the blind side of the referee, then when the ball was centred to him in the air, up would go his hand at the side of his head to propel the ball into the net. He lived in Beswick, a well known character in the pubs and clubs in the district, and was known by many locals as Tommy Alecan. I don't know how much truth there was in it, but it was strongly rumoured that his wife used to bash him, sometimes giving him black eyes.

Philips Park and Clayton

Mark Philips, born 4th November 1800, son of Robert, had advanced Liberal views. In 1844, at a meeting in the Town Hall to inaugurate the purchase of land for Public Parks, he donated £1,000 towards the buying of three estates. The Larkhill Estate (Peel Park), consisting of 32 acres, was bought for £5,000 from a Mr William Garnett; Hendham Hall (Queens Park), 30 acres, from Jonathan Andrew at a cost of £7,250, and Bradford Estate (Philips Park) from Lady Houghton – 31 acres costing £6,200. All were opened to the public on 22nd August 1846, the first public parks in the Manchester area.

I spent some happy hours on spring and summer days in Philips Park and its surroundings. There was the nearest grass to my home in Wellington Street, an oasis in a thickly-populated, garden-less industrial district. We had a choice of three ways to the park. First, we could walk up Grey Mare Lane, passing Cuss's the printers, Tommy Ralph's scrap yard, Bradford Pit and Richard Johnson & Nephew's wire works, where we would look through the open door to see men at machines or stacking bundles of

The day before Tulip Sunday in Philips Park, 1936

wire. A short distance beyond Philips Park Road, a sharp turn right would bring us to the park gates facing the Alexandra public house. Another way was to turn right out of Grey Mare Lane on to Ashton New Road, then at the corner occupied by Latewards the chemists, with the United Hotel opposite, turn left into Mill Street. About half a mile along Mill Street we came to the Stuart Street entrance of the park, close by St Paul's Church. The third route was along Ashton New Road, past the Manchester Slate Company, Clayton Aniline, "Clayton Alps" at the rear of Schofield's Chemical Works, then left into Bank Street at the Derby Arms. We passed the site of Newton Heath's football ground, passed the Corporation Washhouse and Stuart Street Electricity Works and entered the park close by the railway arches.

When in Philips Park we children were in another world, oblivious to the belching smoke from the Stuart Street Power Station and the huge gas holders of Bradford Road Gasworks which loomed up over the park boundaries. The River Medlock flowed through a red brick culvert between the park and cemetery and this always puzzled me. I imagined all rivers had grassy banks like the Mersey I had seen at Northenden. We used to try to scare one another with tales about the Black Hand Gang, Scuttlers or the Ikey Boys. There always seemed to be coal wagons on the railway arches at the Bank Street end of the park, and we believed those gangs lurked amongst the wagons, ready to pounce on unsuspecting boys to "press-gang" them into joining their ranks. It was good, insofar as it kept us well away from the railway track.

Close by the Bank Street bridge

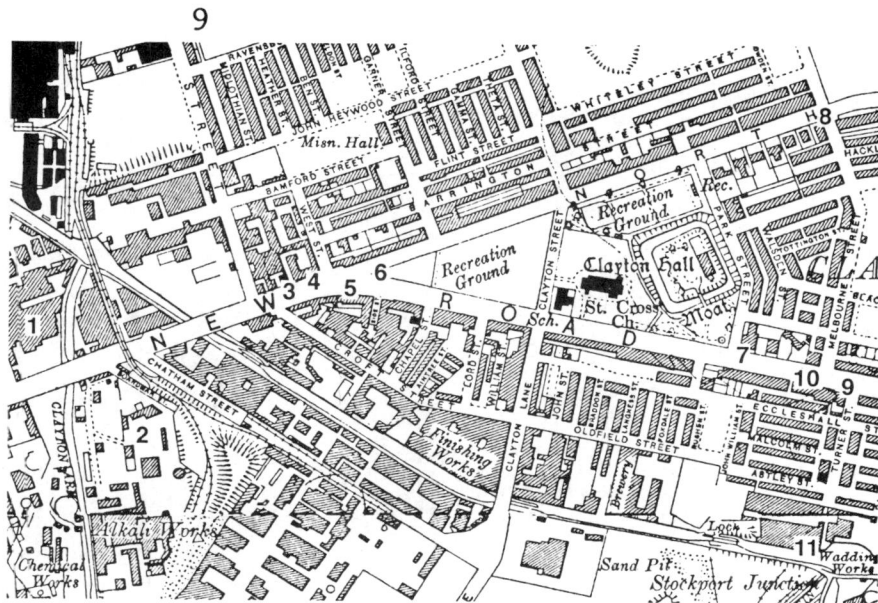

Clayton Hall area: 1 Clayton Aniline. 2 Schofield's Chemicals. 3 Clayton Methodist Church. 4 Charlie Roberts' shop. 5 Sir Humphrey Chetham pub. 6 Public lavatory. 7 Clayton Conservative Club. 8 Clayton Labour Club. 9 Greens Arms pub. 10 Clayton Co-op. 11 Clayton Wadding Company.

was the way on to the Dingle, yet another adventure playground of my childhood. Unfortunately I didn't see it as my dad had known it in his boyhood because rubbish tipping had been started a few years earlier. Ashes and cinders from thousands of house fires, together with coal dust, slag and cinders from Bradford Pit and local industries were used to fill the Dingle in preparation for the building of the Clayton Estate.

Just after the War there was a coal strike. Coal was then a vital commodity to householders for heating and cooking, so stocks soon dwindled. My mother sent me to the Dingle with a large sugar sack to pick coal from the tip. When I arrived, I was astonished to find hundreds of people already hard at work, some with bags half filled with small coal, coke and even cinders. I managed to gather enough to carry that day and Mother was

very pleased. So much so, that I had to go again next day, when I found more people than the day before, some with picks and shovels, digging and picking, and staking claims as in the Klondike gold rush.

Part of the Bank Street end of the tip had been levelled off to make two football pitches. Clayton Rugby Club played on one and Bradford Junior Unionist football team on the other. Since my dad played for Bradford JU, I enjoyed Saturday afternoons watching both teams.

Much of the Dingle was still covered in grass, particularly the steep slopes down to the Medlock, which flows through Clayton Vale. Down in the Vale, on the riverside, stood the Smallpox Isolation Hospital. It was isolation in more ways than one; the nearest property on the Clayton side was in Vale Street, and on the Newton Heath side, the Nunnery at the end of Culcheth Lane. Between the hospital and Clayton Bridge, where the river was reasonably clean with a sandy bottom, boys used to paddle and sometimes swim.

The greatest day of the year for Philips Park, without a doubt, was "Tulip Sunday". It was usually the first or second Sunday in May and it was a beautiful sight, with thousands of tulips of various shades displayed in beds. People flocked from all parts of the city and surrounding areas in their Sunday best clothes to parade around the flower beds. There would be parents with their children, playing on the grass, feeding the ducks or licking an ice cream cornet as they came through the gates.

The 1921 Miners' Strike - children gathering coal at a Manchester pit.

Ice cream carts were not allowed in the park but it was common to see four or five carts busily selling their wares outside all three park gates.

On Briscoe Lane, between Philips Park Cemetery and the railway line, was a football pitch. In the early 1920s Bradford Parish played there and I remember one Saturday afternoon seeing a certain Jimmy Hanson, who had been attracting scouts from many of the professional clubs. He was a local lad who made good, playing for Manchester United for several years as an inside or centre forward. A leading goal scorer, he was very popular with the Old Trafford crowd until a serious injury put paid to his career.

Clayton Hall was the home of Humphrey Chetham, who died there in 1653, and my first sight of the Hall left me with a lasting impression. Here was real history, so near to my home in Bradford. A genuine Elizabethan house with a real moat, surrounded by hundreds of terraced houses and smoke-belching factories. Rarely did I go near Clayton Park without having a look at that charming spot. Although I craved to look round the Hall, I think I was mostly attracted by that moat. Years later it was drained and replaced with concrete and this saddened me. How dreadful! Concrete in a historic setting seemed to me like sacrilege.

The day I discovered Clayton Hall I was on my way to visit friends of my parents who lived

Sir Humphrey Chetham, Ashton New Road

in a house that had been a shop in Stanton Street. On my way I passed the Sir Humphrey Chetham public house, which lay back slightly off the road, with cobble stones in front where carters left their horses while they had a pie and a pint. Very often, a horse would be feeding from a nosebag. On the opposite side of the road was Clayton Methodist Chapel and a few doors away was Charlie Roberts' tobacconist's shop. Now Charlie Roberts, in my dad's opinion, was the greatest centre half who ever kicked a ball. He was a member of the pre-war Manchester United team, the pivot of a terrific half back line – Duckworth, Roberts and Bell. Roberts was one of my boyhood heroes and whenever I passed that shop I used to glance in, hoping to catch a sight of the famous man, but I never did. On the apex of the triangle formed by the junction of Ashton New Road and North Road were lavatories, shrubbery and a red shale recreation ground with a single football pitch, used on Saturday mornings by the local schools, Ravensbury Street and Seymour Road. Between the "red rec" and Park Street was St Cross Church, schoolroom, graveyard and Clayton Park. The park had no playing fields and very little grass, but to my delight, all summer, or so it seemed, there was a beautiful display of Virginia Stock.

At the Ashton New Road end of Park Street was Clayton Conservative Club, with the Greens Arms facing on the other side of the road. This was another carters' calling place, set back off the road with a cobbled frontage.

Clayton between the wars was a very different place from the Clayton of today. On Sunday evenings, North Road was one of Manchester's many "monkey runs". After church on Sunday evenings, youths and girls would walk slowly up and down North Road, from the junction with Ashton New Road to Vale Street and Melbourne Street, wearing their Sunday clothes, weighing up form and figures and endeavouring to get into conversation with whoever took their fancy. In those days anybody who was "courting" was envied, especially by girls, and I am sure many life-long friendships, and marriages, matured through some of these chance meetings.

Clayton Hall and its moat

Belle Vue and Thereabouts

In 1836, John Jennison, a Stockport handloom weaver, acquired a whitewashed cottage in Hyde Road, Gorton. It was opened as a tea garden and small zoo, with a few parrots and monkeys. From such small beginnings, Belle Vue expanded and developed into the wonderful pleasure gardens and zoo I knew during the early part of this century. The spectacular firework displays, with actors depicting historic battles and epics; the great ballroom; the boating lake and the large open-air dancing board delighted thousands of day trippers from Manchester and the surrounding towns. "Day trippers" is something of a misnomer, because Saturday was only a half day holiday in those hardworking years.

As a young boy, living where Wellington Street joined Grey Mare Lane, I looked forward to Saturday afternoons between Easter and the end of September, when a steady stream of horse-drawn wagonettes wended their way along Grey Mare Lane towards Belle Vue, full of happy waving trippers. If we boys thought nobody was looking, we would jump on to the back steps of the wagonettes and ride for a few hundred yards, or until somebody spotted us and cleared us off. Sometimes we had a ride past Barlow Street and Grey Mare Lane Market, to "deck off" outside the Prince's Picture House and go into the little fairground behind the high fence at the side of the cinema to watch, with a little envy, people enjoying themselves on the swings, big swing boats, cake walk, or throwing wooden balls on the coconut shy. We had no money to go for a ride on anything. "Saturday pennies" had been spent on gobstoppers, stickjaw or swaggering dick earlier in the day.

Another adventure on the Belle Vue route was the day three playmates and myself went fishing. It was a hot sunny June afternoon when we set out with penny fishing nets and empty jam jars to catch jack-sharps in a stream in the fields beyond Belle Vue. It being Saturday, we did think about "decking on" one of the wagonettes on Grey Mare Lane, but we were badly handicapped by the fishing nets and jam jars. So on we tramped, past the market, the "Prinnie" and the Grey Mare Hotel into Pottery Lane. Just beyond Crossley's Gas Engine Works, a 53 tramcar rumbled under the low bridge of Ashburys Railway Station on its way to Belle Vue and beyond. We heard a train coming, so we dashed up the stone steps to the platform to wave to the passengers as it steamed through the station on its way to Belle Vue Station at the back of Gorton Town Hall.

Back on Pottery Lane, we passed the Pineapple Inn and the Gorton Brook Hotel at the corner of Clowes Street, to enter Belle Vue Street. Passing Gorton Library and some allotments on the left, we arrived at the Belle Vue main entrance on Hyde Road. People were coming out of the pubs, alighting from tramcars, a couple of wagonettes were arriving and crowds were passing through the turnstiles. Walking along Hyde Road, past Gorton Park and Gorton Baths, we turned right at the Lake Hotel. Then a few yards along an unpaved road (now Mount Road), where the trams turned round to get back to town, and we were in open fields.

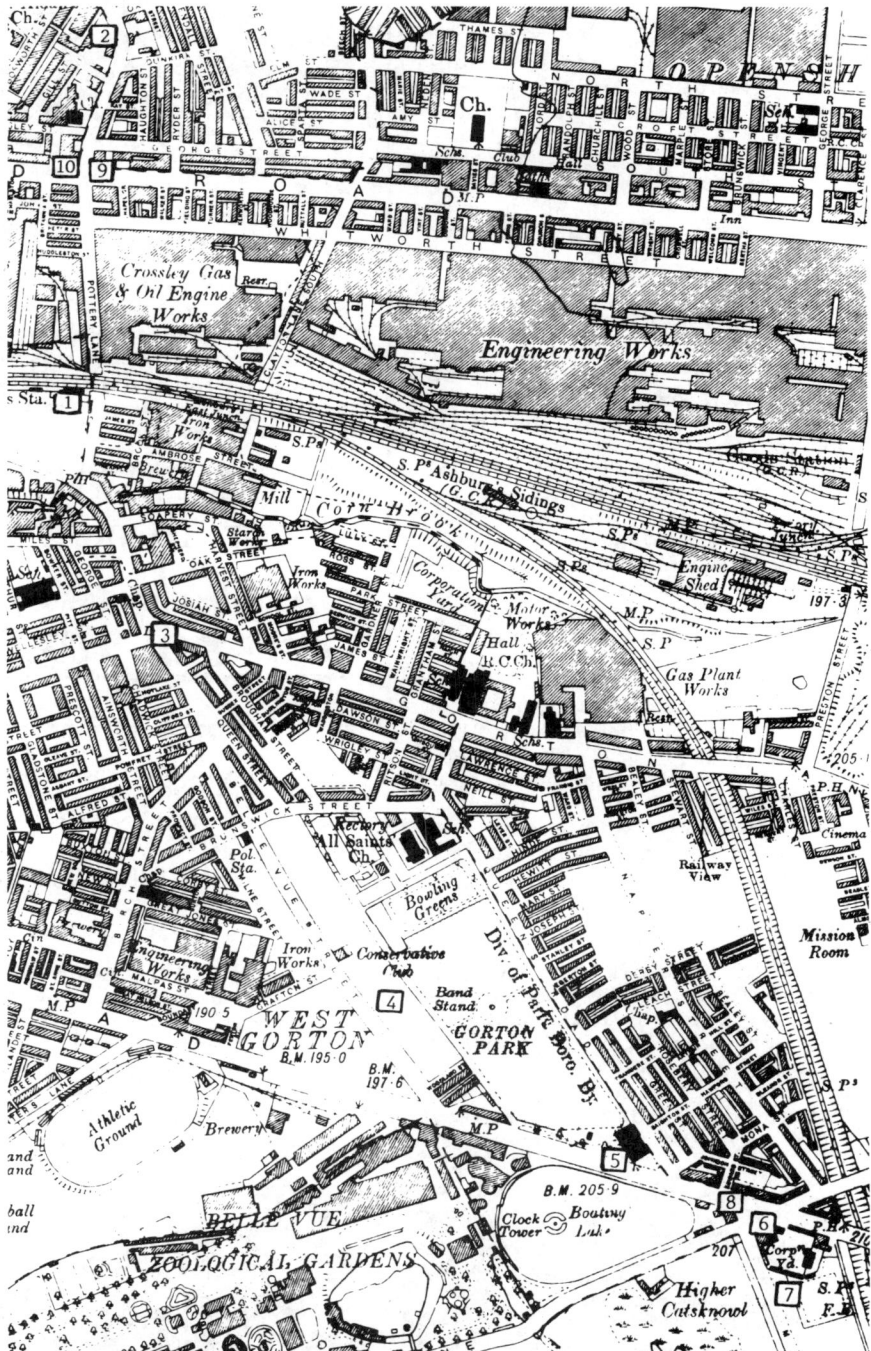

Ashton Old Road to Belle Vue: 1 Ashburys Station. 2 Prince's Cinema and fairground. 3 Gorton Library. 4 Allotments. 5 Gorton Baths. 6 Gorton Town Hall. 7 Tram Terminus. 8 Lake Hotel. 9 Grey Mare Hotel. 10 Burton Ballroom.

It was amazing; so near to the hurly-burly of the Belle Vue traffic and crowds, yet we were surrounded by fields, trees and hedgerows. We pranced through the long grass, shouting gleefully, and quickly finding the stream, we searched for fish. "Let's go further upstream," said Billy Benson, after a few minutes' fruitless search. So we ran to a spot where some trees shaded the stream from the hot sun, and started drawing our nets through the cool water. No sign of a single fish. Undaunted, we wandered off to a small pond on the other side of the field. "Hey! Look here!" cried Tommy Benson on reaching the pond ahead of the others. "Look, there's hundreds of baby fishes!" He was right, so we thought at the time, but after catching a dozen or so each, Arthur Millard, who was older than the rest of us, declared that the jacksharps darting hither and thither in our jam jars were in fact tadpoles. "Let's put them back in the pond," groaned Billy. "I'm not," said I defiantly, "I'm taking mine home." These were the first "fish" I had caught in my life, and I wasn't going to be denied the pleasure of proudly showing them to my mother. Before leaving, I caught a frog, and put it in with the tadpoles.

Arriving home, I put my jam jar on the living room table and sat down to await Mother's reactions when she had finished serving in the shop. Mother entered the room all hot and bothered. Saturday was a very busy day; the weather was hot,

she was tired and there were another three hours to go before she could think of closing the shop.

"What the devil have you got there?" she bellowed.
"Tadpoles, and a frog," I meekly replied.
"Take them off the table immediately, you're not keeping them in here."
"I'll put them in the backyard," I said, reaching for the offending tiddlers. Mother beat me to it. She snatched up the jar, saying, "I'll deal with them. I'll put them somewhere." I followed her into the backyard, wondering where she intended putting my first ever catch. She went straight into the WC, emptied the jar and pulled the chain. I could have cried, but I didn't. I rarely did. It was a sad ending to my first fishing trip, on what had been a happy day in the sunshine and fields.

This happened in the summer of 1919, when most of the land between Belle Vue Station and North Road, Longsight, and between Kirkmanshulme Lane and Matthews Lane, Levenshulme, was open fields. From 1921 much of the land was taken over for the building of Manchester Corporation's second great housing scheme; the first was the Anson Estate in the Birchfields Road/Dickenson Road area of Longsight.

Even in summer, I was sent to bed no later than 9.00pm as a general rule. Anyhow, I didn't mind, because I was usually tired by that time. Then there was the Belle Vue fireworks display which could be seen from the bedroom window. If you looked up Wellington Street in the direction of Ashton Old Road, you could see the rockets bursting in a colourful spray above the house tops.

Greyhound racing, as a public spectacle on a commercial basis, was started in England at Belle Vue on 24th July 1926. Tracks at the White City (Old Trafford), Albion (Salford),

At Belle Vue Zoo in 1923

Snipe (Audenshaw) and Rising Sun (Hazel Grove) quickly followed, but have long since shut down. Greyhound racing had its heyday between 1930 and 1950, but public interest has so diminished that Belle Vue, the first, is the one remaining track to survive in Manchester.

To appear on the bill at the great King's Hall, Belle Vue, was the ambition of hundreds of hungry fighters abounding in the Manchester area in the 1920s and 1930s. The great champions and well known local boxers I saw at this then famous venue included Jackie Brown, Johnny King and Jock McAvoy, all from Harry Fleming's Collyhurst stable; at a later date came Benny Lynch, the dynamic Scottish flyweight, and Peter Kane, the bantam-sized blacksmith from Golborne.

Belle Vue was undoubtedly a wonderful pleasure place for the working people from miles around during those hard times. However, I remember two things frowned upon and frequently joked about by the locals. First was the Belle Vue beer. It was Truman's of Burton-on-Trent. No doubt a good beer to drinkers who had acquired the taste for it, but not liked by the locals who had been brought up on the excellent Manchester brews. People said Belle Vue beer was badly kept and it was very often referred to as "monkey piss". I also remember people poking fun at a mode of dancing called "Belle Vue pump handle style". The gent gripped the lady's right hand, held it down at the side of his left thigh, then as the steps of the dance proceeded, he moved it up and down.

We Move House

In November 1920 my parents sold the shop in Wellington Street and moved to a little house at 33 Park View, Harpurhey. Park View, at the side of Queens Park, is on the borders of Collyhurst, Harpurhey and Cheetham, so we adopted "33 Park View, Queens Park, Manchester" as our address.

Recollections of the flitting are still quite clear, especially the moving to the new address of our moggie, Pongo. One of Mokey Taylor's large horse-drawn removal vans was loaded with our scant furniture, which took up less than half the available space, leaving plenty of room for Mother and brother Arthur to ride with the flitting. I was left with Dad to complete the transfer to the new tenant.

We were about to leave when I noticed Pongo sitting disconsolately in the backyard. I grabbed him, held him to my chest and followed Dad to the 53 tram stop at the corner of Cross Street. The tram came and we sat on the open air seats at the driver's end. I was happy; not unusual for me, for this was a new adventure into the unknown. The tram started to move and so did Pongo. I tried to hold on to him but the strong, frightened pussy burst out of my arms and sprang off the tram into the roadway. On hearing the commotion, the driver brought the tram to a halt and I jumped off, shouting and chasing poor Pongo. Fortunately, I soon caught him and carried him back to the tramcar. Dad was waiting on the steps and said, "Put Pongo under your coat. Hold him tight to your side; that might quieten him." "Hurry up, settle down, can we go now?" said the friendly driver. We were quickly on our way again, along Grey Mare Lane, Forge Lane, Hulme Hall Lane and Queens Road to arrive at Rochdale Road, where Pongo, Dad and myself alighted with some relief. We crossed the road, passed the Milan Inn and a shop at the corner of Peduzzi Street, turned right into Pickup Street and then left into Park View. The house in which I was to live for the next nine years was the second on the row.

I soon settled in and made new pals with the many children round about. But not so poor old Pongo. The poor thing looked as miserable as sin, as Mother would say, and after a day or two decided he'd had enough and slung his hook. We looked everywhere for the poor moggie, under the beds, in the coal hole, the backyard and the closet. After searching the surrounding streets and alleyways, Dad said, "I wonder if he's found his way back to Wellington Street?"

Imagine my delight, that Saturday afternoon, when we found Pongo sitting on the doorstep of 22 Wellington Street, disconsolately looking at the passers-by. It was apparent that his return to the shop had not been a very happy one, but he was certainly pleased to see Dad and me again. We put him in a box with air holes, tied it with rope so that he couldn't see where he was going, and off we went back home. I am pleased to say that Pongo never strayed again.

We had little furniture to start with at 33 Park View. In the front bedroom where Mother and Father slept was the iron bedstead with brass knobs, a dressing table with three

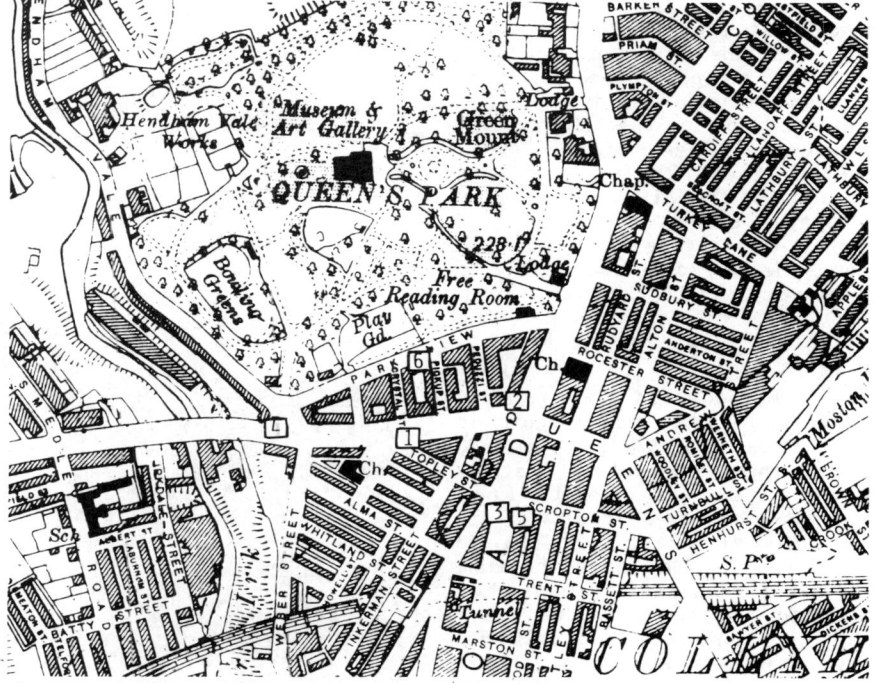

Queens Park and Neighbourhood: 1 Queens Arms. 2 Milan Inn. 3 Balmoral Hotel. 4 Junction Hotel. 5 Gem Picture House. 6 33 Park View

drawers and a marble-top washstand with the usual jug and bowl; all bought from the second hand shop. There was only a bed in the back bedroom, where my brother and I slept. In the front room downstairs was a plain, unpolished dining table, four wooden chairs and, believe it or not, a piano, made by Steele Higgins of Green Street, off Tib Street, Manchester. The dark, flag-floored kitchen was simply adorned with an old wringing machine with large wooden rollers. On Sunday dinner and tea times we had a white tablecloth, but during the week a couple of sheets of the Manchester Evening News had to suffice. Nevertheless, we were quite well fed, although Arthur and I had to fend for ourselves six days a week. Mother always saw there were plenty of vegetables, salad greens and a good selection of fruit in the house.

Mother got a job as an assistant in a pork butcher's shop in Alexandra Road, Moss Side, which entailed her leaving home about 7.30am and not returning until nearly 10.00pm. Dad didn't get home from work before 6.00pm each evening, so we boys were left to our own devices for much of the time, especially during school holidays. This afforded us ample opportunity for adventure, discovering the landmarks and interesting aspects of the new environment.

Queens Park Faces and Places

First of all, I made the acquaintance of the local boys and found them an amiable bunch. Ernie and Herbert Band, Mick (Malcolm) Campbell, George Walker and Alfie Walker (no relation) all lived in Park View; Harry and Billy Thompson lived in Pickup Street, Bobby Wood lived in Sydenham Street and Reggie Burns in Crystal Street; these were the first of my playmates in the district. They readily accepted me into their circle and I think I became fairly popular. Whether it was because I had a full-size leather football, a bat, a ball and wickets, or that I introduced swimming as a popular pastime to them, I will never know. Anyhow, it was tit for tat; they introduced me to the fun of "guidering". I was fascinated, and soon pestered Dad into constructing one of these guiders for me. It consisted of a board about 3'x18" with two wheels at the back and two smaller steering wheels at the front. Park View and Hendham Vale were built on a fairly steep incline, so three or four of us would drag our guiders up to the library at the top of Park View and then sit on them for a nice long ride down the hill. The flagged footpath along by the park wall was rarely used by pedestrians, so we were able to ride along Park View and down Hendham Vale to where the River Irk flows by the footpath - great fun!

The neighbourhood was rich in characters. The first to come to my notice was "Dicky Madden", my teacher in Standard 3 at my new school. I don't know whether he ever realised it, but he was known as "Ten To Two Feet" by the boys, because of the angles of his feet when walking. I used to wait for Dicky passing our house on his way to school and then I knew it was time to have a cat lick and make tracks myself.

Very often, especially in the wintertime, Dicky would talk to the class with his back to the fire, against the big iron fireguard. At times he gave the fireguard an almighty kick with his heel, and at the same time raised his voice to a shout. The boys soon discovered this antic was to cover for his breaking wind. Some boy would whisper, "Hey! Dicky's just farted!" and a chuckle would start on the front row, then spread throughout the class, with Mr Madden shouting, "Quiet boys!" at the top of his voice.

Ice Cream Johnny was another character. He always wore a cloth cap (I think he was bald-headed) and a red muffler round his neck. He kept a small wooden hut on Queens Road, facing the Junction Hotel and adjoining the bridge over the River Irk, next to Hinchcliffe's toffee shop. Johnny sold hot chestnuts in the winter, and the world's worst ice cream all year round. It was absolutely tasteless! It was a penny a glass - a thick-bottomed glass which deceived the eye into believing that you got about twice as much as you actually received. Nevertheless, there always appeared to be somebody sitting on the forms, passing the time of day, licking the tasteless stuff and chatting to Ice Cream Johnny.

Drunken Johnny was a lodger at a house in Park View. I think he worked on nights, which allowed him, after a few hours' sleep, to spend all lunchtime hours in the pub. His red hair made him very conspicuous when he staggered and swayed his way home in the afternoons. It was mostly during school holidays when we came across Johnny, and very often children would shout to him, "Drunken Johnny! Drunk again!" then run away to a safe distance. Johnny would turn, shaking his fist, and would threaten in the foulest language imaginable.

In the early 1920s Micky Hamill, the Irish international and Manchester City half back, lodged at a house in Park View, a few doors away from where I lived. Whenever I saw him, I would gaze at him in awe; he was like royalty to me. I delighted in telling the lads at school that Micky

The fountain, Queens Park

Hamill lived near me. It didn't make me any better a player, although I'm sure it did inspire me a little in my efforts on the football field.

Yet another well known character in the Collyhurst/ Miles Platting/Harpurhey area was "Nancy Dickybird". She acquired the name because of her beautiful singing voice. I never heard her real name. She was a reformed drunkard who sang with that remarkable institution, the Salvation Army. But occasionally she would "break out" and go on the booze, frequently causing a disturbance, to be escorted to the police station by a friendly local Bobby who had probably taken care of Nancy several times before. I only saw her drunk on one occasion, so my memories of Nancy are mainly of her singing in Topley Street and going into the Balmoral Hotel at the corner of Rochdale Road and Collyhurst Road to sell the "War Cry".

Mr Hargreaves, my piano teacher for more than three years, was a loveable character whom I greatly admired. He lived on Queens Road, between Smedley Road and the railway bridge, almost facing the generating station. He was an elderly, retired gentleman, teaching to earn a few shillings to augment the ten shillings national pension of those days. I don't think he had any diplomas - his qualification was a lifetime's experience in music. He had been a choirmaster and organist in his native town of Bolton and was a teacher of singing and organ. I never saw him not wearing his cloth cap, so I presume he was bald-headed. I can picture him now, sitting beside me, wearing a clerical grey suit and, of course, his cap, occasionally stroking his grey moustache, pointing out something on the music sheet with a long knitting needle. Being a sentimental so-and-so, I still retain and value the reference he gave me when I ceased lessons with him.

The Albert Memorial Church, and particularly the adjoining Albert Memorial Croft on Queens Road, have happy memories for me. Smedley Road School football team used to play matches against the Albert Memorial School on Monsall Recreation Ground. The Albert Memorial Croft was the home ground of Mount Tabor, a successful amateur football team. On Saturday afternoons well over a thousand spectators thronged the touchlines, and the pitch they played good football on consisted of crushed cinders, marked out with sawdust.

Park View to Cheetham Hill Road: 1 Smedley Road School. 2 Tin Tabernacle. 3 Cheetham Hill Congregational Church. 4 Finnigan's Dance Hall. 5 Generating Station. 6 Junction Hotel. 7 Ice Cream Johnny's. 8 Barney's

The Albert Croft was also the fairground for Pat Collins's Wakes three or four times a year. We looked forward to Pat Collins's Fair - to sit in the pea saloon on a winter's night, warming one's hands on a large cup of steaming hot black peas, was a never to be forgotten experience. It cost a penny for a cup of black peas and water, boiled with more than enough pepper and salt, which made the mixture taste hot.

The boxing booth was good fun, providing you kept out of the ring! There always appeared to be a crowd outside, listening to the patter and banter of the man trying to entice any mug who fancied his chance with any of the booth's bruisers. He would challenge anybody to last three rounds with any one of his boxers the challenger would choose. If by chance he survived the three rounds, he would receive the princely sum of £1, a prize not to be sneezed at in the 1920s. When some bold chap put up his hand, he would be thrown a pair of boxing gloves. The three booth boxers would each be paired with an opponent and the crowd would surge into the booth after paying a small entrance fee. The fee varied, depending on time of day and day of week; Saturday night was usually dearest.

On the left of Queens Road, between the railway bridge over the busy Bury electric line and Cheetham Hill Road, was rough open land with no buildings except the church we called the "Tin Tabernacle" and the brickworks way over towards North Street. This area was known as Barney's, a name derived from the one-time owners of the brickworks. To the local lads this was a natural adventure playground, where we played cricket and football, rode bicycles and watched and waved to the trains. With the approach of Guy Fawkes Day, our search for bonfire wood would take us to Barney's, where we usually found at least a couple of old railway sleepers. We would tie ropes round them to drag them to store in somebody's backyard in Park View.

The kilns at the brickworks were the well known haunts of tramps, especially on cold winter's nights. Periodically, the police would have a raid on the brickworks, and once arrested 35 tramps sleeping rough without visible means of support.

The tram depot, an extensive red brick structure, was about 20 years old at that time and still looked surprisingly new. Close by was Finnigan's Dancing Academy, where I made my first faltering steps in dancing at the age of 14.

Like most boys, I was always fascinated by the sight of water, so the nearness of the River Irk attracted me and my pals to further our adventurous pursuits. Access to the river banks was easy; either through the passageways off Hendham Vale, or by climbing the fence in Weber Street. On the Weber Street side of the river was the

Devil's Path, a narrow track about sixty or seventy feet above the river. In wet weather, to walk this path was a precarious and dangerous feat. Some lads did it, but not me. I was the world's worst tight-rope walker - I couldn't walk along the top of a wall without falling off. The opposite bank was flat, with some factory buildings close to the water's edge. One of the buildings had a corrugated iron roof and we thought it great fun to throw stones down across the river, to clatter on what we called the "tin roof". After a short time, an angry man would emerge, shaking his fist and threatening to inform the police. So that would be the end of that bit of fun, and off we'd go in search of some other form of entertainment.

In contrast, the Hendham Vale length of the river was fairly flat, with a steep, grassy bank on the opposite side. At the rear of the houses on Hendham Vale was a large pigeon loft, where I went on several occasions to help my school pal, Victor Bebbington, retrieve his wayward birds. I think one bird in particular found a mate there. In the end Victor got so fed up with continually bringing his bird back whenever he let it out that he sold it to the owner of the loft for 1/6d.

Near the pigeon loft, along the river bank, was a shed about 50 yards in length where rope was made. At this point, in summer, the river was shallow enough for us to wade across. The bed of the river was stony and hard on the feet, but the worst sensation was when you felt your foot sink into a dead dog or cat. Once over the river, we would make our way past the farm, round by Smedley Hall and into Smedley Lane, where Kennett House flats now stand. Then past the S M Shirt Company, across the bridge over the Irk, turning right at the Smedley Hotel into Hendham Vale, and we were nearly back home.

After school on Fridays was the time for doing the weekly shopping, so off I would go with my list to Hugh Fay's, Meadow Dairy, Maypole Dairy and Walton's greengrocer's on Rochdale Road to fill my two baskets. Sometimes I would buy half a pound of dates for "afters". The dates were on the greengrocer's counter in a compressed block, about a one-foot cube. I remember asking my father why dates came to the shops like that and he told me it was cheaper, needing less materials and labour. Then he went on to explain how the natives in Africa picked the fruit, threw it on to a cart, and then when the pile got to a certain size, they trampled on the dates until they were thoroughly compressed and the natives almost exhausted. What a tale! And I believed him - for a short time, anyhow.

In the mid 1920s, Manchester had a kind of festival of arts and entertainment called Civic Week. On the Saturday I was going on an errand to Boots Chemist, next to the Gem Picture House, facing the Balmoral Hotel on Rochdale Road. I knew all the short cuts, so instead of turning into Rochdale Road at the corner of Steele Higgins' piano shop, I turned into Inkerman Street, then into the back entry which would bring me into Topley Street. Suddenly, I was confronted with a strange sight. Somebody had been "taken short", to part with the largest "George the Third" I had ever seen. What first attracted my attention was the notice some joker had stuck on the huge dollop, so I stooped to read its message. "DO NOT DISTURB. CIVIC WEEK SOUVENIR". Laughing all the way to Boots, I got the thing I had gone for confused. Instead of asking for a bottle of Sanderson's Specific, I asked for Canadian Pacific. The assistant laughed, and laughed; I went red, and redder. That afternoon, I took several of my mates to the spot at the side of Weatherby's Bakery to view the "souvenir", because they thought I was kidding them, exaggerating the size of that great turd.

I have fond recollections of the Wednesday evening band concerts in Queens Park. At that time, after football, cricket, swimming, camping, walking, discovering and eating, history and music were my favourite interests. Bands were in the park on a dozen Wednesdays during the summer, so on those

Crumpsall Biscuit Works

Pendleton Public Prize Band

occasions I put aside my other interests to stand as near as possible to the bandstand and thoroughly enjoy the playing of such bands as East Manchester Military, Pendleton Public Prize, Gorton and Openshaw Silver, and Culcheth Top Hat Band.

The S M Shirt Works and the CWS Biscuit Works were two outstanding landmarks in my boyhood, simply because the fields in between were the scene for many happy hours of playing and watching football, cricket and other pleasurable pastimes. At the rear of the Biscuit Works field was a small reservoir where we caught newts and frogs and then matched them in races, but with little success. The field at the side of the S M Shirt Works belonged to Frost's Farm on Smedley Lane, and the field in front was also grazing land for farm cattle. A fresh water stream divided the S M field from Cawley's Playing Field. From that same stream we gathered watercress, which we ate on the spot. The open air always made us hungry. I don't really know whether it was real watercress, but it tasted like it. In fact, we said it tasted better than that from the greengrocer's. The funny thing was, we regularly "wee-weed" in the stream and claimed that as the reason for the exquisite taste of the "watercress".

Between Cawley's Playing Field and Small and Parkes' Works, Hendham Vale, the Irk flows sluggishly on its way to join the Irwell. The reservoir and Irk were favourite spots for playing skimming with any stones we could find. After two or three hours playing football or cricket, growing boys naturally began to feel rather peckish, so we would make our way to the Biscuit Works. "Hope we can see that chap who wears the brown smock," somebody would remark. "Aye, he gives us a lot more than the other man," I would shout. If we could catch the man in the brown smock, we got a large bag of broken biscuits for a penny - if we could muster a penny between us.

Cawley's Playing Field had three full-size football pitches, and was the home ground for Smedley Road School's football team's league matches. What a thrill it was on a Friday, after school, to walk through the streets with the school's red and green hooped football jersey draped over my back, with the sleeves tied round my neck. Then on Saturday morning, turn out from home in full football kit, hoping my pals would see me, to walk all the way to Cawley's.

When not playing myself, I would watch Collyhurst Recs on Cawley's, or British Dyestuffs, who had a good team, on their enclosed ground on Hazelbottom Road. My favourite player in the Dyestuffs team was a man called Aldred. He was a very good amateur, considering he had a handicap of a withered arm, which must have affected his balance considerably.

Topley Street Methodists played cricket on Cawley's. I was interested in them because I knew some of their players, including two of the Wood sons from Sydenham Street. However, the best cricket team, attracting most attention on Cawley's, was a team from Cheetham Hill called "Red Rose".

My inquisitiveness soon prompted me to explore the territory beyond the tram sheds, so I wandered up Elizabeth Street, past the Jewish Hospital, Waterloo Hotel and across a croft on St James Road (where at a later date I played football), across Leicester Road into Tully Street, up Northumberland Street, and then found myself in Great Clowes Street at the Cliff. This section, long since closed because of land erosion, gave a good view of the Irwell, Kersal Vale and Manchester Racecourse. A short distance away was Broughton Rangers' Rugby Ground, which brings to mind a New Year's Day when I watched the rugby match and the horse racing from one end of the ground which looked down on the river and on to the racecourse. The races were run at half hourly intervals and many of the spectators, especially if they had had a bet, would make their way to the top of the banking behind the goal, which afforded a splendid view of the racing. Not far away, near a public house called the Priory, was the football ground of one of Manchester's leading amateur teams, McMahon's.

Smedley Road School

Smedley Road School, opened 5th June 1882, was one of Manchester's earliest elementary schools. It was built high up on the Cheetham bank of the Irk, fronting Smedley Road. It was a mixed school, with the senior classes occupying the large hall, divided by a glass partition, and two classrooms at each end on the upper floor. The Infants' Department, Standard 1 and Standard 2 were on the ground floor. There were two playgrounds, one for the girls and infants, the other for senior boys. At the top of the boys' playground was a corrugated iron structure used for woodworking and cookery classes. When I first attended the school, although it was less than 40 years old, it was blackened by the soot and grime of industry and smoke from domestic chimneys.

My brother Arthur started his schooling there in the infants' class, and I was placed in Dicky Madden's class, Standard 3. Mr Roberts was the headmaster at first, but after a short time he was transferred to Moston Lane and a Mr

Manchester Racecourse - a foggy January day in 1923

Scholes was appointed. I soon settled to the new routine and slowly progressed in all subjects. The bright boys sat on the back rows and the not so bright sat on the front row. Having very poor eyesight, I always had to sit on the front seats in order to read the blackboard and because of this, some of the boys got the mistaken impression that I was a bit of a dunce. With grim determination, I soon proved I wasn't, especially in sporting activities.

Being interested in the geography of Manchester led me to a thirst for knowledge of local history, so the Monday afternoon sessions at Queens Park Museum stimulated an interest that has been with me all my life. At the end of the summer term we had an examination and I once received top marks. My reward was the choice of a miniature replica of one of the pictures in the Art Gallery. My favourite at that time was "The Last of the Garrison", so I chose that. Was I proud? I certainly was! It was framed and hung in my bedroom alongside the "give-aways" and newspaper cuttings of football and cricket teams from the Adventure, Rover, Wizard and Sunday newspapers. I think my priceless prize was left hanging on the wall when we flitted to Woodleigh Street, Blackley.

Another lesson which I found very interesting was the Friday morning session in Standard 7 on First Aid, or "ambulance lesson", as we used to call it. I think we were most fortunate in having a teacher who was a St John's Ambulanceman, a little man named Mr Whalley, who taught us the names of the bones in the body, blood circulation and how to render First Aid with bandages and splints.

Although I wasn't much good at it, I enjoyed the woodworking class - "manky" (manual), we called it. The building was used by other local schools such as St Oswald's, Forest Street; Albert Memorial and Collyhurst Municipal - known locally as the "Tin School" because it was a corrugated iron structure. The woodwork teachers were Mr Wood (what a coincidence) and Mr Dewar, who had a turned-up nose and so was nicknamed "Ringy". The best model I made was a cheese cutter, but when I took it home Mother said she would rather use a knife. How ungrateful, I thought, after all my effort! But never mind, I might make something useful next time.

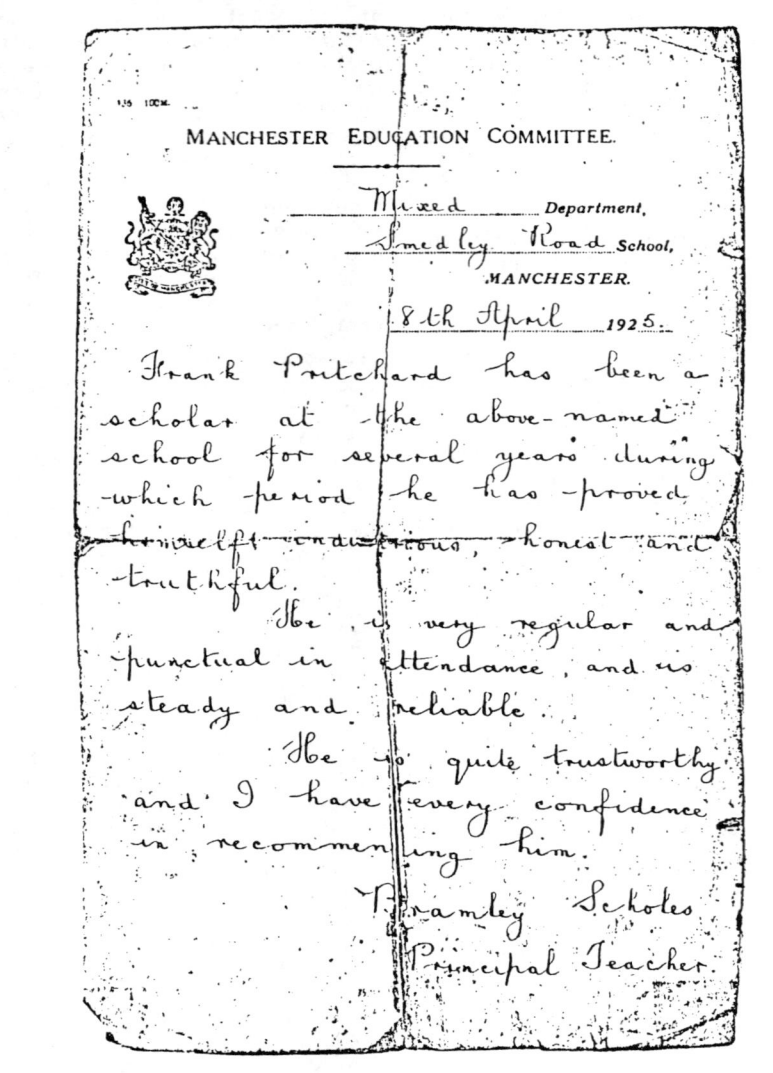

My favourite master at Smedley Road School was Mr Stubbs, teacher of Standard 5. He had a little waxed moustache and pince-nez glasses and he reminded me of what I thought a Frenchman would look like - I imagined him to be of French extraction. Unlike some other teachers, he never seemed to lose his temper, although he always managed to maintain strict discipline through his personality and good humour. On entering a noisy classroom, he would shout: "Now you boys, make less noise; you'll spoil the joys of other boys."

Mr Harper, Standard 6, was easy going, unruffled, but strict and well-respected. He was, I think, in his mid-forties, experienced and mature. The fact that he was sportsmaster gained him much popularity with many of the boys, me included. He was in charge of the football and cricket teams and his friend, Mr Moore, a teacher at St Augustine's School, Monsall, was a prominent member of Manchester Schools' Football Association. Mr Harper also had a friend who was a racehorse trainer at Newmarket. In my class was a boy, small and underweight for his age, who on leaving school had ideas of becoming a jockey. Mr Harper took a personal interest in him and got him a job as a stable lad and apprentice jockey at Newmarket. This was typical of Mr Harper, but unfortunately the boy grew, and grew, to become too heavy for a jockey, and had to be content with being a stable lad.

Mr Whalley, teacher of Standard 7 and X7, was nearing retirement age. Apart from First Aid and gardening classes, he was a good all-round teacher who had learned the knack of making most lessons interesting. However, I hated him after he made me the butt of his misplaced humour in front of the class by calling me Rip Van Winkle. If the writing on the blackboard was too small, I experienced great difficulty in reading it, even from my position on the front row. On one occasion, when gazing at the blackboard, I must have had a blank look on my face. Unfortunately, Mr Whalley spotted me, pounced on me with some questions, and of course I was unable to answer, which prompted him to shout, "You were asleep, boy, weren't you?" adding, "You're a Rip Van Winkle, the man who slept for twenty years!" A couple of days later he addressed me as "Rip Van Winkle", so I ignored him. He could see I resented his bad mannered approach and asked, "Can't you read what's written on the blackboard, Pritchard?" I explained as best I could that the writing was too small, and with a puzzled look he carried on with the lesson.

A fortnight later I hated him much more; my parents received a letter from the Manchester Education Committee, summoning me to attend at their Deansgate offices, with the alarming prospect of being taken into the care of Henshaw's Blind Institution, then commonly referred to as the "Blind Asylum". I was distraught. "They can't do that to me," I moaned to my mother. "They say they can, but don't worry, I'll come with you," she assured me, which comforted me to a certain extent. The vital day arrived; Mother took the morning off work and we arrived at the Deansgate offices, wondering what fate would determine my future. I knew my mother was a tough little woman who wouldn't be cowed by anybody and would fight tooth and nail on my behalf. She explained to the three-man committee that she was quite happy with my progress at Smedley Road School, that I was an energetic boy who played football and cricket successfully, in spite of wearing glasses, and was able to read music proficiently. I was asked questions to verify the truth of Mother's statements, then the three men went into a huddle, quickly came to a decision that I would be able to find my way through life and that my eyesight wasn't as poor as had been reported, and said they were sorry we had been unnecessarily troubled. My confidence had been justified; it was a wonderful relief.

Down Rochdale Road

As a schoolboy, I was interested in reading the school stories of Frank Richards in the Gem, Magnet and Popular. I was also very fond of boiled sweets, gobstoppers, aniseed balls and swaggering dick, all of which could be bought cheaply at the Crescent Market. The market was held on a piece of ground facing St Oswald's Church on Rochdale Road, between Churnet Street and Collyhurst Street. Rochdale Road in the 1920s was a busy thoroughfare, lined with shops, public houses, churches, picture houses and schools, well provided with tramcar services and even a railway line crossed the road from the Oldham Road Goods Depot to the Manchester Corporation Gasworks. On my way to the market I would pass the Gem Picture House, where I frequently attended the "first house" showing for 2d. The Gem was on the corner of Scropton Street; at the next corner, Trent Street, was a big greengrocery shop near the Picturedrome, which was locally known as the "Jews". I don't know why, because I believe the proprietor was a Greek. At the corner of Alexandra Street was a doctor's surgery, and at the corner of Churnet Street stood the Three Tuns public house. Then came the Crescent Market, with naked flare lamps lighting the various stalls on Saturday nights. People would crowd round the greengrocery or the "pot" stalls, listening to the patter of the stallholders, hoping to pick up a bargain. Back issues of "blood and thunders" such as Sexton Blake, Magnet, Gem, Boys' Magazine, Popular, Dixon Brett and Nick Carter could be bought from the bookstall for ½d each.

The market site was later occupied by a cinema, but I doubt whether it ever gave as much pleasure to folk as the Crescent Market. It didn't to me - I never went in the place. The Gem, Jews, Queens Park Hippodrome in Turkey Lane and the Princess in Conran Street were nearer; there was also a market by the side of the Princess.

Beyond the Crescent Market, towards town, you came to Collyhurst Street with Salt's grocery shop on the corner, and a few doors along the row was a doctor's surgery over which one of my school chums lived; his parents were caretakers. Facing Collyhurst Street was Warren's toffee shop, where another boy from Smedley Road School lived, and next door, in an old factory, was St Malachy's Roman Catholic Church. Further along Rochdale Road, looking down the next street, one could see St James's C of E, and along the following block on Rochdale Road the well patronised premises of May's pawnshop. In Gay Street, at the rear of the Crescent Market, was the well known Dicky Banks's "bug hut". I never did hear the proper title of this picture house, as most people knew it only by its nickname.

The streets off both sides of Rochdale Road were lined with small, two up and two down terraced houses, many of them overcrowded with families of eight or more. At the corner of Osborne Street was the Osborne Hotel, and a few yards along the street the Osborne Baths, which before the 1914-18 war was the base of the Osborne Swimming Club, one of the best water polo and swimming teams in England. Close by the

Amateur Swimming Champion J H Tyers, of the pre-war Osborne Swimming Club

Osborne Hotel was the most famous pawnshop in Manchester, Piggy Riley's, a vital institution in this densely populated district of Collyhurst. On the opposite side of the road stood a home-made boiled sweets shop. When the sweets were being made, a delicious smell greeted you as you passed the shop. At the end of the row was Dalton Street, with a little cinema facing the railway wall where the trains disappear under Reather Street bridge. A few yards beyond Reather Street was Binks's junk shop, full of second-hand paraphernalia, and opposite was a row of houses with stone steps outside, leading down to cellars in which people lived. The windows were about three feet above ground level, but the gaslight seemed to be on in daytime, even in summer. Between Reather Street and Livesey Street was Abbott Street School, one of Manchester's first free schools, built by the School Board and opened on 12th August 1878. The school had a well-earned reputation for its prowess in producing many really fine swimmers. Opposite Livesey Street was a public house known locally as Tommy Cassidy's. The landlord's son, a schoolteacher, played centre forward for Manchester United. From Livesey Street to the block of dwellings where the railway waggons crossed the road carrying coal supplies to the gasworks was waste ground where old property had been demolished. In later years the Rochdale Road Bus Depot was built there.

Between Thompson Street and Swan Street was Shufflebottom's pottery warehouse, and between Addington Street and Cable Street stood the premises of Veritas Gas Mantles. At the Corner of Swan Street was the Rising Sun, with its large flagstone-floored concert room where many of the old music hall artists appeared before the war. My dad told me that Dan Leno and Wilkie Bard had **performed** there in days gone by.

On the opposite side of the road, at the corner of Angel Street, was the wholesale hardware warehouse of Binns Ltd. Next door was Travers and Pierson, basket and cane furniture makers, where I once worked for six months alongside my father. Looking through the rear windows, we could see into Kane's Lodging House in Angel Street, a notorious place where the homeless down-and-outs and criminals could get a meal and a bed for the night for a few pence. Also at the rear was the old established firm of Baxendales Ltd. In those days they boasted a fine brass band, and when we worked late, we enjoyed their playing on practice nights.

In and around Smithfield Market

The area of the town surrounded by Shudehill, Swan Street, Oldham Street, Church Street, High Street and Nicholas Croft was an extremely interesting and lively part of Manchester. It was exciting to visit the market on a Saturday afternoon or night to join the crowds shopping and be entertained by the spiel of the stallholders and the music of the buskers. The "quacks" bawling and shouting, trying to persuade people to buy their "cures for all ailments"; the man on the "pot stall" tapping a "jerry" with a toffee hammer, making it ring to prove it wasn't cracked, and the men with barking dogs for sale in Tib Street or Oak Street all added to the commotion and fun. There were the ice cream carts, the boiled sweets stall, and the second hand bookstall with people browsing, hoping to pick up a bargain.

After darkness, the inside market was lit by gas-mantled lights, but outside stalls were illuminated by acetylene flares. The market was open until 9.00pm, and about 8.30pm many shoppers could be seen hanging about round the meat, fish, fruit and vegetable stalls, when perishable foods were sold at "giveaway" prices before closing time. Every weekday the wholesale market was busy from 4.00am onwards, tapering off towards noontime, then the market workers turned their attention to the many pubs in the vicinity, where some of them stayed until "kicking out" time.

The Wheatsheaf Hotel in Oak Street had a special licence to open at 6.00am for the benefit of the market men and traders and the George and Dragon at

The Hen Market and the old Rovers Return

the corner of Swan Street and Oak Street, if it could speak, could tell some hair-raising tales. It had a reputation for being a rough "dive" and I understand they had "chuckers-out" - big chaps who could adequately deal with trouble-makers. During the last war it was a favourite place for men in the forces. About that time, the pub became known as the "Band on the Wall", because music was provided from a small balcony rather high on the wall. The Smithfield Vaults was another pub favoured by the market fraternity, and nearby was the Cosy Corner Cinema, where the audience consisted mostly of either weary market men having a well-earned rest or drunks sleeping off the booze before daring to go home.

In the market area, in a little street called Green Street, was the workshop of John Steele Higgins, piano makers. When I was 14, instead of wanting to be an engine driver, I fancied the idea of an apprenticeship in piano manufacturing. One Saturday morning I was in Smithfield with my dad when suddenly he said, "Hey! There's Steele Higgins. You'd like a job there, wouldn't you?" Before I had time to reply, he pushed me through the doorway into the works, saying, "Go in and see if they need an apprentice." A man in a black apron approached; I could not retreat, so I blurted out, "Do you want any boys?" I think he was only a work-man, and he was soon joined by three others. Leading me to one of the pianos, he said, with a grin, "Can you play that?" I don't know whether they expected me to struggle through some memorised light classical piece on the dilapidated instrument, but I sensed an element of surprise when I belted out a couple of choruses of a popular song of the day, "Ukelele Lady", which sounded absolutely great on that "honky tonk" piano. The men smiled with admiration and said, "We'll let you know." But even at the age of 14, I knew what that meant. They had no vacancies; I think they simply intended having a bit of fun at my expense, but it wasn't quite what was expected.

In Turner Street, off High Street, was the warehouse of Fred Aldous, cane importers, where I used to collect bundles of cane for my father. He would give me a note ordering several six-foot lengths of malacca, bundles of reed cane and willow. He also gave me tram fare, ½d each way, from Queens Road corner. But I was never able to get on a tram with my bundle - the trolley boys seemed to take a delight in pushing me off whenever I attempted to board one. So I was always forced to carry my awkward burden about a mile and a half to Park View.

In the 1920s and 1930s, Shude-hill and Withy Grove were busy, interesting thoroughfares. At the Nicholas Croft end, facing the Hen Market, was Pifco Ltd, one of the first electrical equipment suppliers in the city. Near to Dantzic Street was a well known saddler's and leather goods shop. In the early 1920s there were far more horse-drawn vehicles than motor powered and that shop was still doing good business in harnesses in the 1930s. On the other side of Shudehill were the stalls of the Hen Market, with the centuries-old Rovers Return in the middle of the row of shops behind. In 1924 the Rovers Return was an antique shop, but gradually fell into decay and after stand-

Manchester Flower and Vegetable Market

Street traders in the Shudehill area, 1920

ing empty and unused for many years was finally demolished in 1959. I have happy memories of the old Hen Market, where they sold not only hens but also rabbits, white mice, guinea-pigs and puppies. On one occasion, I went with my father to buy "day-old" chickens, and to my delight he bought me a large Belgian hare.

Near the corner of Garden Lane (Garden Street) was the site occupied by the old established firm of Greene and Calvert, a jewellery, watches and fancy goods warehouse and shop. Between Garden Lane and Corporation Street were Berisford's sugar merchants and the Old Boar's Head. As I write this, I can relish the taste of the dark, sweet "best mild" beer for which the pub was renowned. The brewery was Adshead's of Macclesfield, who also had the White Bear in Swan Street.

On the corner of Swan Street and Shudehill, facing the Rising Sun, was Duncan's pipe makers, a famous name to pipe smokers. A pal of mine worked there as an apprentice and he used to show us younger boys, with much pride, the brown stains on his fingers made through his job of staining and polishing the pipes.

Further along Shudehill beyond the Hare and Hounds, at the corner of Thomas Street, stood the premises of the old established firm of Brooks, wholesale chemists. On the opposite corner was Lockhart's Cafe, a favourite eating house for the local office and warehouse workers; very few firms had canteens at that time. At the other end of the row, on the corner of Nicholas Croft, was William Lindop's sports outfitter's shop, where I once purchased a set of 12 football shirts for our boys' team, Crystal Athletic, for £1 2s 11d.

In the middle of the row was the Lower Turks Head (still standing), one of the many Walker & Homfray pubs in pre-war Manchester. Undeservedly, in my opinion, Walker & Homfray's beer was frequently referred to as "Water and Comfreys" by the seasoned drinkers, especially those who had been weaned on Chesters' renowned "fighting beer". Between the wars, quite a large number of breweries thrived in the Manchester area - names such as Kay's, Boardman's, Holt's, Swales', Threlfall's, Hyde's, Chesters', Gartside's, Boddington's, Openshaw Brewery, Groves & Whitnall's, Manchester Brewery and Wilson's offered the drinker a far wider choice of brews than can be obtained today. Wilson's, always a progressive firm, had one of the best advertising campaigns I can remember. Lots of hoardings on walls, spare land and lining the main roads afforded much space for billposter advertising. Suddenly, besides the usual posters advertising the merits of Colman's Mustard, Sunlight Soap, Fry's Cocoa or Lyons' Tea, there appeared huge yellow and black draught boards, without any printed information whatever. The blank draught boards were also printed in the local newspapers. The public was intrigued. In the streets, pubs, clubs, shops and on tramcars, folk could be heard asking, "What are all those draught boards about?" People realised it was an advertising stunt, but for what? It was a closely-guarded secret that kept people guessing for some time. Then just as suddenly as the baffling draught boards had appeared, words were added informing the public that the draught boards indicated where the finest beer was obtainable – Wilson's houses. The secret was out, Wilson's was on everyone's lips, and I'll bet their sales received a considerable boost.

Along Thomas Street, on the left hand side towards Oldham Street, between the well known public houses, the Bay Horse and the Millstone, was the old established drapery and furnishing firm of Woollerton's. My mother never tired of singing their praises for reliability of goods and service. Before reaching the English Leather Shoe Shop at the corner of Oldham Street I would pause at the shop windows of Oates', the tool specialists; they sold tools of the finest quality.

Next to the Swan With Two Necks in Withy Grove was Kemsley House (Thomson House), known to most Manchester people as the Chronicle Office, where the Evening Chronicle, Sunday Chronicle, Empire News and several weekly and periodical publications were printed. Many Mancunians will remember placing their 12 results football coupons in the special letter boxes at the Chronicle Office. This was a free competition; a prize of £500 was awarded to the person or persons who could correctly forecast 12 results. Coupons appeared in the Football Chronicle on Saturday nights, and in the Empire News and Sunday Chronicle. The losing team was forecast by crossing out their name in ink; draw forecasts were left open. It was an extremely popular competition – £500 was a fortune, especially to the thousands of unemployed and low paid workers in those hard times. It would buy a newly-built house and completely furnish it.

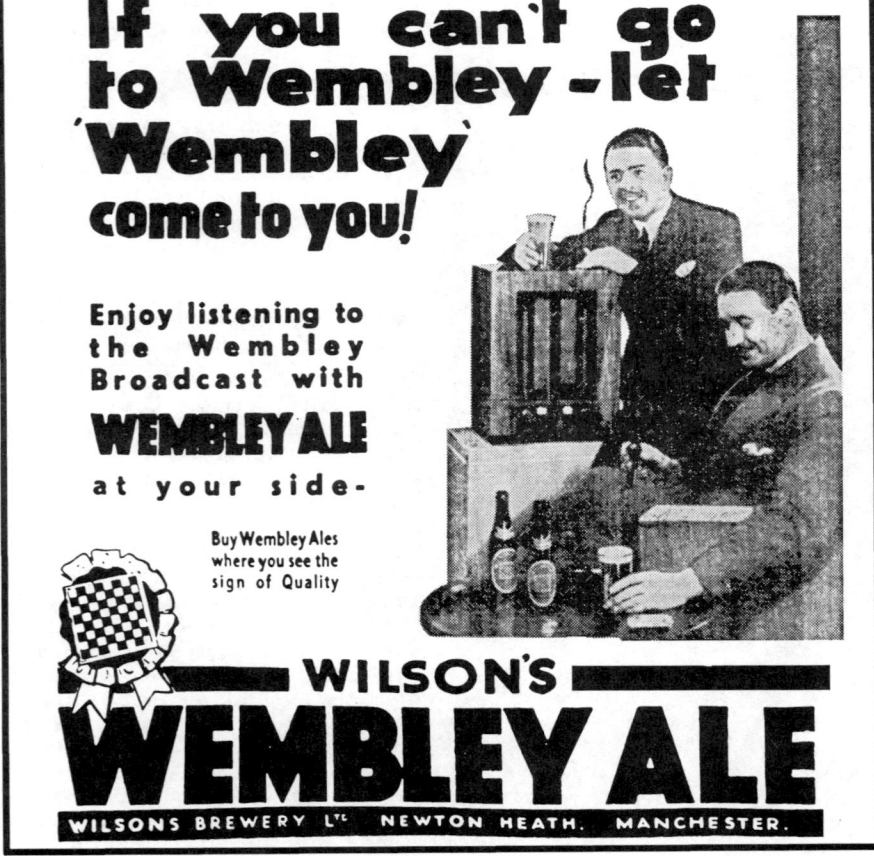

Wilson's Brewery advertisement in 1934 - the year City won the FA Cup

Miller Street and Balloon Street

In the 1920s Miller Street could have been more fittingly renamed Baxendale Street. Most of the property on both sides of the street was occupied by the firm known all over the world. In 1870 the street was mostly occupied by old building material brokers and Marine Store dealers, but by the first years of the twentieth century Baxendales had taken over. Laban Baxendale (1832-1908), a glass-cutter by trade, sacked by the small firm he worked for because he requested to become a partner, started a business on his own account in Hanover Street, with a credit of £100 from Pilkington Brothers of St Helens. A few years later, Baxendale was joined in partnership by Henry Gordon, who undertook the travelling; a Charles Darrah took charge of the counting house and Mr Baxendale kept control of the buying and general management.

The firm moved to Miller Street in 1869 and from then on expanded by leaps and bounds to gain a world-wide reputation by the 1920s. Branches were opened in Liverpool and Edinburgh and there was a finely equipped works in Trafford Park. The various departments supplied all kinds of building materials and furnishings. When the move to Miller Street was made there was a staff of 40, but by the 1920s the firm employed well over 1,000.

Between the wars, Baxendale's boasted one of the best brass bands in the North of England and gave excellent performances in the Manchester parks, greatly appreciated and enjoyed by the citizens. Several of Baxendale's buildings were badly damaged by bombs during the war.

Baxendale's, dominating Miller Street

The only other building of note in Miller Street was the Union Cold Storage Company at the corner of Dantzic Street, but we cannot leave Miller Street without mentioning the first steam-powered cotton mill in Manchester, which stood opposite the Union Cold Storage in Factory Yard, on the corner of Dantzic Street and Miller Street, until it was destroyed in the Blitz of 1940. In 1783, Richard Arkwright was responsible for the building of this steam-driven cotton mill, which speeded up the production of cotton goods in the closing years of the eighteenth century. The mill was badly damaged by fire in 1854, but was rebuilt to last for another 86 years.

Miller Street was certainly a hive of industry during the 1920s, with carts loading and unloading along both sides of the street. The roadway was often blocked by the slow-moving traffic, resulting in the 51 tram (Miller Street to Brunswick Street, Oxford Road) being delayed quite considerably on the journey along this narrow thoroughfare and the even busier Swan Street, especially in the early morning. I had to walk from Swan Street to Great Ducie Street on my way to work, and sometimes it was a dodgy job evading the carters and loaders as they carried their wares across the footpath.

At the corner of Miller Street and Corporation Street, the Ducie Bridge Hotel, facing the CIS building, was the terminus for the 51 tram. Turn left on to Corporation Street, passing Mayes Street, and one comes to the fine building housing the headquarters of the Co-operative Wholesale Society at Balloon Street. In 1868 the CWS, one of the more important commercial undertakings associated with Manchester, took possession of a small warehouse in Balloon Street. Rapid expansion resulted in a series of fine buildings covering an extensive area, including the splendid administrative block facing on to Corporation Street. The CWS had a good reputation for being wonderful employers, and any boy or girl securing a job there was said to have a "job for life". Recruitment was mainly restricted to school leavers, and a steady job with security was the aim for parents of most children in those hard, competitive times. Most posts were filled by recommendations from friends or relations already employed at the CWS - "Somebody to speak for you," as envious people used to say.

Further up Balloon Street, at the corner of Dantzic Street, was Royle's wholesale boot and shoe warehouse. The continuation of Balloon Street is Bradshaw Street, and a few yards up this street on the left was the warehouse of the wholesale footwear firm, J & E Smith & Co Ltd. On the opposite side of the street is the old Castle and Falcon, where I sometimes called for a "quick 'un" after a day's work, before making my way to Piccadilly to catch the bus. The corner of Shudehill, facing Lockhart's cafe, was occupied by Cardwell's string and rope shop.

Manchester's first steam-powered cotton mill in Factory Yard

Harpurhey and Blackley

Harpurhey and Blackley were exciting places in my younger days. We went rambling through McKenna's Wood (now known as Bailey's Wood), over Charlestown fields, Blackley Golf Course, and fields surrounding Victoria Avenue East. There were happy "camping out" days in Rhodes Wood (Alkrington Wood, what there is left of it); cricket, football, rowing and running in Boggart Hole Clough, and dancing at Blackley Palais, Harpurhey Conservative Club and Harpurhey Baths. There were some cinemas to be enjoyed, such as the Blackley Empire in Factory Lane, the Victory in Charles Street, the Princess in Conran Street and the Avenue on Rochdale Road, near to Victoria Avenue. I favoured live theatre, and greatly relished many of the shows at the Queens Park Hippodrome in Turkey Lane.

Leaving Park View at the library end and turning left on to Rochdale Road, you passed Smith's piano shop and the Jubilee Chapel on the right, then on the corner where Conran Street branched off to the right was the site occupied by Burgon's grocery and provisions shop. Continuing along Rochdale Road past the Harpurhey Cemetery, past the Derby Hotel and Burgess Street School on the right, Drinkwater Street and Foresters Arms on the left, you arrived at Central Avenue (Harpurhey Road). A few yards further on stood the Golden Lion and, a short distance away, we sometimes saw the fire engine coming out of Ash Street Fire Station. Beech Mount was the 1½d stage for the 17 and 18 tramcar routes from High Street, and either trolley boy or conductor would shout, loud and clear, "Beech Mount! Anybody for the Maternity Home?" The cheeky ones would shout, "Anybody for the Pudding Club?" I think it has now been replaced by a clinic.

On a spare piece of ground at Beech Mount in the mid-1920s was the Blackley Palais de Danse. In fact, it was in Harpurhey, but I think the proprietors thought "Blackley" sounded posher. As a lad of 14, I was lucky enough to attend the opening night at the new dance hall. It so happened that a cricketing pal of mine, Granny (Granville) Hinchcliffe, had secured a job as junior reporter with the Blackley and Middleton Guardian on leaving school. He was detailed to cover the opening of Blackley Palais, so he took me along for support. Being aware that I had been to Finnigan's Dancing Academy on a couple of occasions, he probably thought I knew more than he about ballroom dancing. I had learned a few steps of the waltz and fox trot, but my main interest was the dance band aspect. My lasting impressions of that night were seeing for the first time the Argentine Tango, the One Step (forerunner of the Quick Step), and that the Paul Jones was the most popular dance of the night.

Facing Blackley Palais at the corner of Church Lane was Christ Church, and on the next row of shops was Stiles' Funeral Undertakers (relations of Manchester United and England footballer Nobby Stiles). A hundred yards beyond Moston Lane is Harpurhey Baths, which is really in Barnes Green, Blackley. Between the wars, Harpurhey Baths was a favourite venue for many local people. Apart from the pleasure of swimming there, one could see and appreciate first class water polo games, for in those days, Harpurhey was a name to be reckoned with in top class water polo and swimming circles. They had outstanding players such as Tommy and Freddy Jepson, Alf Downing, Bert Ward, Jack Donoghue, Joe Major, George Bridge, Eric Pendleton and Pete Anderson, to name but a few. Exciting, hard fought matches were played against such teams as Bradford Dolphin, Wigan, Halifax, Hyde Seal, Southport, South Manchester, Manchester Swan, Lancaster and the London clubs of Penguin, Otter and Plaistow United. Most of the Harpurhey swimmers graduated from local schools noted for their prowess in training large numbers of good swimmers - Alfred Street, Mount Carmel, Abbott Street and St Patrick's were the leaders.

During the winter months, the second class "plunge" was covered with a dance floor and was a very popular dance hall. Blackley Palais had a very short life as a ballroom, probably due to the nearness and popularity of Harpurhey Baths Ballroom and the advent of the "Talkies". It was refurbished and re-opened as a cinema under the name of the Palladium. Eventually the cinema declined as profitable entertainment and the building became the Northern licensed club.

A hundred yards or so past the baths, at the gates to the Lewis Recreation Ground, was Blackley Institute, where private dances and functions were held throughout the year. From this point the road goes downhill, shaded by large trees

The author's parents at Douglas, Isle of Man, in 1927

Fun and Games

in Boggart Hole Clough and on high ground bordering Mount Carmel Church. This section was known as the "Vall" (Valley), or the "Monkey Run". Boys and girls would stroll as far as Charlestown Road or Blackley Tram Office, then turn to walk back, sometimes repeating the walk several times. Then if they had not "clicked", they would turn into the Clough to join the crowds listening to the band, hoping for better luck there.

Boggart Hole Clough was to my mind the most natural and prettiest park in Manchester. The lake and fishing ponds were sited on the highest point in the park, where the air always appeared to be clear and fresh. What could be better than the pleasure and healthy exercise derived from a couple of hours' rowing on that lake? Perhaps a few laps round the running track, or a couple of hours listening to a good brass or military band could be better. Anyhow, it was all there; a grand exhilarating place, far removed from the drab back streets of Miles Platting and Collyhurst.

Beyond Blackley Tram Office, open land bounded both sides of the road until Alkrington, on the outskirts of Middleton, was reached. McKenna's Wood and the Jewish Cemetery on the right, then a few houses and shops on the Manchester side before Victoria Avenue, were the only properties before our camping paradise, Rhodes Wood, came into view. I remember, every time we passed the Jewish Cemetery, one of the boys would say, "That's where they bury 'em standing up, so they'll have a quick start on Judgement Day, when it comes."

On the left side of Turkey Lane was Queens Park Hippodrome, where I spent many mid-week winter evenings. The price of a seat on the long forms in the rear stalls was 3d, and what good value it was! Queens Park Hippodrome was one of the Broadhead Circuit, a chain of local theatres which included the Metropole, Ashton Old Road; Kings, Stockport Road, Longsight; Salford Hippodrome, Cross Lane; Osborne, Oldham Road; Hulme Hippodrome, Preston Street, and the Crown, Eccles.

Many of the stars of those days started their theatrical careers at those local theatres. I well remember a young comedian at Queens Park Hippodrome in the early 1920s. Because of weight problems, he had recently abandoned the idea of becoming a jockey to try his luck on the stage. That young hopeful became one of the country's popular performers, George Formby, who on that occasion was billed as "George Formby Junior". Two other famous comedians I saw there in hilarious revues were Sandy Daw and Albert Burdon, who was in a funny show called "On the Dole".

During the pantomime season some of the young stage girls attended Smedley Road School and although we boys thought them "stand-offish", we sometimes went to see what they were like in the show. On one occasion, two of us went as far as trying to meet some of the girls at the stage door after the show. We did manage to have a few admiring words before they were whisked away by their chaperon. Anyhow, we were quite happy, not having been snubbed, and the comedian had a friendly chat with us. I remember he sang a nonsensical parody of one of the songs of the day, "Ukelele Lady". The first line was: "Kiwi, Nugget, Cherry Blossom, Nugget, Cherry Blossom, Kiwi" - names of shoe polishes; silly, but it fascinated me.

There was a change of show every week, which meant the pantomime girls attended a different school every week during December and January. It must have been quite bewildering to the youngsters. The established, well-known artists usually played the city theatres such as the Palace, Hippodrome and Ardwick Empire, but on occasions top variety turns were only too glad of a week's work at the Queens Park Hip. Which brings to mind names like Billy Bennett, "almost a gentleman"; Billy Russell, "the English working man"; Albert Whelan, the eloquent, immaculately dressed Australian, and Harry Weldon, with his comedy goalkeeping act. Albert Whelan was reputed to be the first artist to use the signature tune "Jolly Brothers" to start and finish his act on stage. I saw all these great turns filling in a week of their diaries at the Queens Park Hippodrome.

Conran Street and Upper Conran Street were remarkable insofar as they did not have a single public house between Turkey Lane and the Moston Lane end of the thoroughfare. Even when a young boy, it struck me as rather strange, because all the main roads had dozens of public houses. Nevertheless, it was possible to get a good pint at a place near St Stephen's Church - the herbalist's - where the boys called after coming out of the Prinny (Princess) to quench their thirsts with a drink of herb beer or sarsaparilla. Sometimes, during the football season, we preferred Vimto, which had recently come on to the market. It was said to be full of vitamins, so we kidded ourselves it was better for footballers in training.

We used to go to the first house at the Princess Cinema (admission to a "plush seat" was 3d) to enjoy the exciting cowboy films of Tom Mix, William S Hart and Buck Jones and the comedies of Charlie Chaplin, Harold Lloyd, Ben Turpin, Charlie Chase, Hank Mann and Buster Keaton. Conran Street Market was on a spare piece of

Boggart Hole Clough - the fountain

ground adjoining the Princess. My favourite stall was the home made boiled sweets stall, where they sold acid drops, pear drops, cough drops, treacle toffee and mint humbugs at 2d a quarter pound, and they were delicious.

Upper Conran Street had mainly red brick terraced houses, of little interest to my young mind. Moston Lane was very different, with its shops and school. Moston Lane School, opened 19th August 1901, was of particular interest; being a school with great sporting prowess between the wars they frequently had the best football and cricket teams in the North Manchester area.

Hough Hall, in Hough Hall Road at the side of Moston Lane School, was the oldest building in the district. I believe some of the timbers dated the hall to the reign of Henry VIII. In 1605 it belonged to the Halgh (or Hough) family; then in 1700 it was the home of the Lightbownes, who eventually sold it to the Minshulls. In 1774, Hough Hall was bought by a Mr Sam Taylor, a prosperous businessman. I was in the building in 1935, when it was my doctor's surgery.

In a little street just before the junction with Kenyon Lane was a cosy little picture house, the Moston Imperial Palace – the Mip to the locals – and at the corner of Kenyon Lane was a well-known landmark, the Ben Brierley Hotel, named after the famous Lancashire dialect writer who lived for many years in Moston. From there, a few yards down Kenyon Lane on the right, was Jimmy Winter's Dance Hall in the Lightbourne Liberal Club, which gave great pleasure to the "dance mad" youngsters of those days, and also saw the start of many romantic involvements. Moston Lane, like most neighbourhoods at that time, had its pawnshop; Ted Shields was the name. He also sold cheap clothing and footwear, and advertised in the Manchester Evening News and Evening Chronicle as "The Cheapest Man on Earth".

At the Rochdale Road end, next to a bank, was the booking office of the best-known furniture removal firm in North Manchester, Makinson's. They also ran popular charabanc trips during the summer to Blackpool and other North West resorts. A public house called the New Inn was on the opposite corner facing, on the corners of Factory Lane, two more locals,

Hough Hall

the Golden Tavern and the Derby, known locally as the "Little Derby", to distinguish it from the Derby Hotel opposite Harpurhey Cemetery. At the corner of Charles Street stood a small public house with a mainly "vault" clientele, which did good trade on match days when Manchester North End was at home.

Manchester North End started life as a successful amateur team called New Cross, before becoming semi-professional at the Charles Street ground. Probably the most famous name to wear their colours was Charlie Broadhurst, the ex-Manchester City centre forward. For a few years the ground was used for baseball, the home of the Manchester Blue Sox. The English style of baseball had been played in the Liverpool area for many years, but the game around Manchester was a new venture to try to popularise the American version. It did not take on, lacked sufficient support and faded out after a couple of seasons. One well known sportsman I remember seeing against the Blue Sox was the great Jim Sullivan, the famous Wigan rugby league full back. He played for Wigan Red Sox, but was no newcomer to the game, having played for a Liverpool team for a number of years. It was unfortunate that the inauguration of Manchester North End coincided with the great slump of the early 1930s. Sufficient support could not be maintained, and the club folded up after a brief existence.

In 1929 my family moved to 11 Woodleigh Street, off Clough Road, Blackley. At that time, Woodleigh Street consisted of one row of terraced houses with a grocery shop at the corner of Clough Road. The road was unpaved, with a fair-sized field in front of the houses and allotments between the end of the street and Goodman Street. Access from Goodman Street was by way of a public footpath, which I think must have been an ancient right of way. In later years, semi-detached houses were built on the field, and Lewis Avenue extended through the allotments to Clough Road. We were delighted with 11 Woodleigh Street, which was undoubtedly a social uplift. Three rooms downstairs, three upstairs, and most wonderful of all, a bathroom, for the first time in my life; it was simply great! Also, it was only a few yards away from my favourite park, Boggart Hole Clough.

One particular freezing, clear, moonlit Sunday night in the Arctic winter of 1929 will live in my memory for all time, when hundreds of people skated and slid about on the thick ice of the boating lake. It was a wonderful sight – boys and girls giggling, laughing and chatting, thoroughly enjoying a rare occasion, and I was lucky to be one of them.

Around Oldham Road

Both sides of Queens Road, Hulme Hall Lane and Oldham Road abounded with life. This was a thickly populated area of working class people with close family ties and wonderful community spirit. Between the ages of 10 and 18, much of my leisure time was spent in these lively localities.

There was always some kind of activity going on. A walk along Needwood Street, Monsall Street, Harrowby Street, Thornton Street or Lodge Street would reveal people making their way to the many corner shops, women hanging washing across the street, children playing games along the footpath or in the roadway, and men sitting on doorsteps watching the world go by. There were always football matches in progress on Monsall Recreation Ground, Hulme Hall Lane Rec or the Albert Memorial Croft.

A team called Egerton Vics (Victoria) drew crowds to the Hulme Hall Lane Recreation Ground. They were a pub team with a formidable reputation, having in their ranks a popular local professional boxer, Boy Armstrong.

The area bounded by Clifton Street, Hulme Hall Lane and Lord Street (now Lord North Street) contained rows of red brick terraced houses owned by Mr Pendlebury, who also owned the tripe works off Grey Mare Lane and a chain of retail tripe shops. A workmate of mine lived in one of those houses, which was familiarly known as the "Tripe Colony". This part of Miles Platting, otherwise a district with many public houses, was "dry", without neither a public house nor an off licence. It was said that Mr Pendlebury, who was responsible for building the estate, was a staunch teetotaller.

Sixty years ago, Oldham Road was a thoroughfare of exuberant activity. Through Collyhurst, Miles Platting, Newton Heath and Failsworth, both sides of the road were lined with small shops, rows of little houses, workshops, mills, factories, picture houses, theatres, public houses, chapels, churches and even a Town Hall at Newton Heath. It stood on land facing Ten Acre Lane and the adjoining building was Newton Heath Baths, where I used to go for a swim on summer's evenings before calling for my chum who lived at Williams Deacons Bank at the corner of Dixon Street.

On my way, I would pass Ceylon Street, with the Ceylon

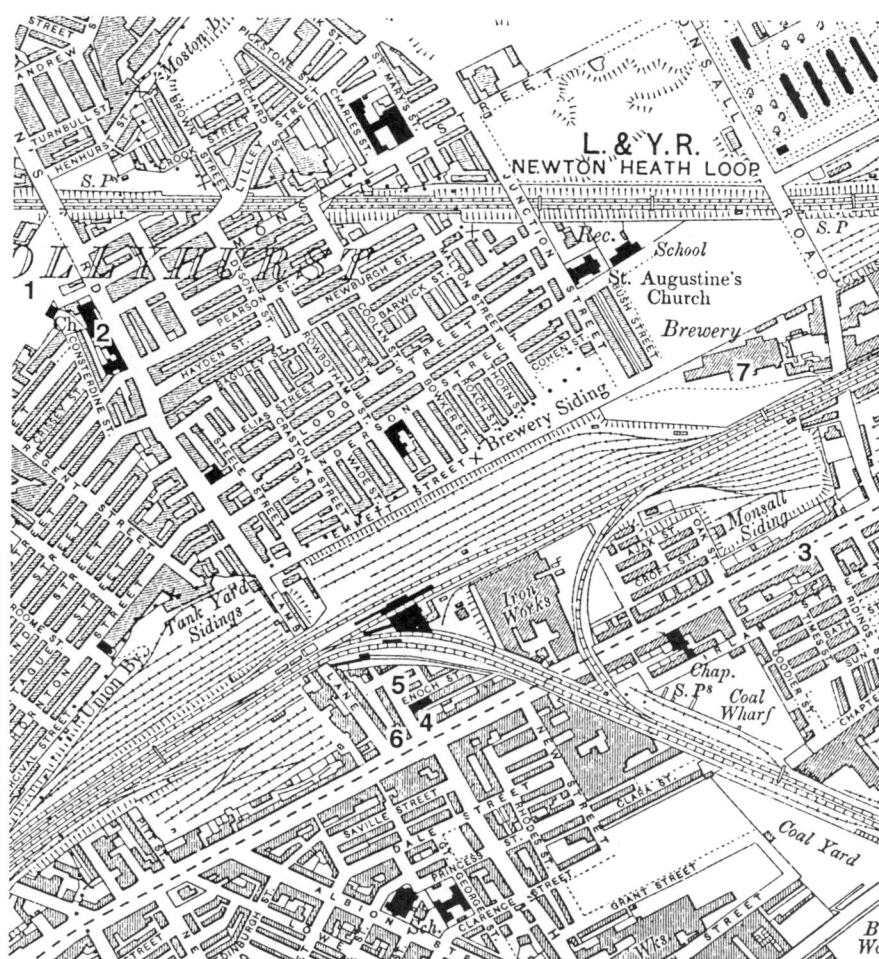

Rochdale Road to Oldham Road: 1 Albert Memorial Croft. 2 Albert Memorial Church and School. 3 Joe Taylor's. 4 Rechabite Hall. 5 Popular Picture House. 6 Playhouse Cinema. 7 Wilson's Brewery.

Picture House, and Newton Heath Loco football ground at the top end of the street. At the Oldham Road corner was Gosling's fishmonger's and greengrocer's. It was there that the tremendously successful local amateur football team, "Gosling's", originated. They started their career in the Manchester Wednesday League, playing against such teams as Pendleton Co-op, GPO, Manchester City Transport and Manchester City Police. Many trophies were won, so the club progressed through the Manchester Amateur League, Manchester League and into the Cheshire League, winning championships year after year. Several first class players started their careers with Gosling's, including Jack Crompton and Henry Cockburn of Manchester United.

Ironically, it is said that the great success of the team contributed to the demise of the Gosling's club. In their heyday they attracted good crowds to their home games, but venturing into higher leagues involved greater running expenses, such as travel, new kit and administration costs. For spectators, the result of games was a foregone conclusion, so watching a team with such winning consistency became monotonous. Crowds dwindled, and with this financial support diminished to such an extent that the club folded up because it had been too successful on the field of play.

Between the Town Hall and Gosling's was Thorp Road, where I had my first date with a girlfriend, attending a concert by the Manchester Police Band in the Newton Heath Loco Canteen.

At the end of Thorp Road, turn left into North Road (now Northampton Road), and on the right was a football ground where Manchester Boys played some of their inter-town matches. A turn to the right out of Thorp Road into Lightbowne Road, then a few yards beyond the Kenyon Lane/Dean Lane junction, close by the newly-built Lightbowne Hotel, was the mineral water factory where my favourite tipple at that time was made - "Pickup's Tizer".

In the 1920s Dean Lane started at Oldham Road and went right through to the junction of Lightbowne Road and Kenyon Lane. It was a short cut to Moston and beyond, soon to be denied to the public by the walling off of about a quarter of a mile of the road by the railway company, thus rendering Dean Lane a "No Through Road". This was a pity, because it denied access to the cinder path frequented by the many courting couples in the district. "Still, never mind, there's still the cinder path off St Mary's Road," couples thought; unfortunately it became a little congested.

From the large Failsworth Co-operative building, now derelict but then a thriving business, past the Pavilion Cinema as far as All Saints' Church, Church Street was a busy shopping street which on Sundays became part of a "Monkey Run" along Droylsden Road to Brookdale Park.

On Oldham Road, almost opposite Monsall Road, was Newton Heath Conservative Club, better known as Joe Taylor's, where dancing took place on the upper floor six nights a week. Another local dance place was the Rechabite Hall on Queens Road, facing the Playhouse Cinema. This fine red brick building has apparently not become a victim of the town planners and it still stands to this day. In a little street at the rear of the Rechabite Hall was the Popular Picture House, known locally as the "Flea Pit". The "Pop" was one of the first cinemas in Manchester. Seating was on wooden forms and admission was 2½d.

Wednesday night was popular at the Ceylon Cinema. Midway through the second house performance an interlude of popular music was played by local dance bands. The favourite band, especially with the girls, was Curly Appleford's.

"Go as you please" competitions were very popular between the wars. They were held one night a week, usually Friday, at many local theatres or cinemas which had a stage. The Grand at Failsworth and the Pavilion and Ceylon in Newton Heath attracted full houses on competition nights, but my favourite was the Playhouse on Oldham Road. There were generally about a dozen turns in the contest, each allowed five to ten minutes for their act. Conjurers, pianists, banjoists, comedians, but mostly singers of varying talents filled the bill. Some were exceptionally

Lightbowne Hotel

good, some were mediocre and a few were simply appalling!

On one occasion in 1922 I went to the Playhouse to support my dad and his partner, a light comedy vocal act, and a small section of the audience had the obvious purpose of giving all turns the "raspberry", with the exception of the act they were supporting. The first four turns were hooted off the stage within seconds of starting their act, so I began to quake in anticipation of my dad's fate. Next came an elderly chap in soldier's uniform, singing "Roses of Picardy". He actually got through his act with slight murmurings. Somebody in the front seats shouted, "Give the poor old sod a chance!"

Next came a rather plump young woman, singing "Love Will Find a Way" at least a semitone out of tune. She got half way through the chorus and the hooting and raspberrying developed into a crescendo. The manager frantically beckoned her to leave the stage, but she carried on regardless. The din was deafening, turning into hilarious guffaws of laughter when the manager crept behind the pitiful soul, put his arms round her middle and carried her off into the wings, kicking, screaming and protesting loudly. It was a pitiful sight, but it raised the biggest laugh of the night. When all competitors had done, or tried to do their act, the judging was by loudness of applause. The acts lined up on stage and the manager went along the line, asking for applause while placing his hands on the shoulders of each one in turn. The prize for the winner was £1; second prize was 10/- and third 5/-. I was really proud when the "Harmony Boys" (my dad and partner) were awarded second prize. At the same time, I was much relieved.

Some of the large pubs had concerts on certain nights (though never on Sundays) with paid artists. Smaller pubs had a "free and easy" room, with a piano of sorts, where anybody could volunteer to entertain the customers. Friday and Saturday nights were busy, lively nights in the congenial atmosphere of the local. Darts, dominoes and crib were the popular pastimes in the "sawdust" (vault), as it was sometimes called, because of the sawdust spread over the floorboards. It was not very inviting to anybody with a fastidious taste, but it had the advantage of cheaper beer - a penny a pint cheaper than the "best room" or "snug" prices - to compensate for the lack of comfort. Mild beer ("Jimmy Wilde", as it was sometimes called), was 2½d a half pint in the "pepper and salt"; bitter beer, on which it was said regular drinkers eventually went raving mad, was 3d a half pint. The best room had oilcloth or lino on the floor, curtains to the windows, and the inevitable "honky-tonk" piano. It was alive with topical conversation, much laughter and the singing of such songs as "Lily of Laguna", "Nellie Dean", "Memories", "Danny Boy" and the latest "pop" songs - "Alice Blue Gown" and "Peggy O'Neil" - and a place where work and worries of the day were cast aside for a couple of hours.

The family removal to Woodleigh Street, Blackley, considerably widened my scope for discovering new landmarks in Lightbowne, Blackley, Chadderton and Moston. A favourite walk, summer or winter, was along

Moston Lane, past the Ben Brierley and the Brierley Hall dancing rooms over the Co-op, past the Blue Bell Hotel, Moston Fields School, the Thatched House pub on the left and St Joseph's Roman Catholic Cemetery on the right, and into Nuthurst Road to Alberti's Cafe at the corner of Lightbowne Road. Alberti's was a meeting place for boys and girls and many a romance started there over a cup of tea or tub of ice cream.

Any reference to Moston Cemetery and I can picture a cold, wet day in January 1927, when I attended my first funeral, that of my maternal grandfather. The funeral cortege, a hearse and three carriages drawn by beautiful black horses, started from St Brigid's, Mill Street, Bradford. We arrived at Moston Cemetery in a blizzard, the burial service was rushed through and we couldn't get back to 323 Mill Street (facing Birch Street and St Brigid's) quick enough. Few words had been spoken, but hot drinks and sandwiches soon loosened the tongues of the mourners. After the meal, out came the whisky. Jugs of beer and stout were brought in relays from the off licence. Jokes and amusing tales were told, Irish songs were sung, and Grandfather was given a really good send off, so it was said. It certainly was an astonishing experience for a boy of fifteen.

Cheetham, Cheetham Hill and Crumpsall

The most memorable buildings in Cheetham were Cheetham Town Hall, the Great Synagogue (opened in 1858), St Chad's Church (opened in 1847), Holt's Brewery in Derby Street, Queen's Road Tramsheds and the one that stood out for both exterior and interior architectural beauty - Cheetham Assembly Rooms, opened in 1860. The interior was one of the finest in Manchester. It had one of the first spring dance floors in the country, perfumed air ventilation, a stage, ornate decoration and attractive crystal glass chandeliers. At the front of the building was a "drive-in", separated from the traffic of Cheetham Hill Road by ornamental wrought iron railings, which enabled carriages to unload guests attending functions at the steps to the entrance.

In January 1927 I had the thrilling experience of attending my first ball in this exquisite ballroom. It was the occasion of Timpson's Annual Staff Dance. I did very little dancing, but I had a lovely night, listening to the dance orchestra playing to a crowded floor and gazing in wonderment at the scene. One tune I remember the band playing, for a one-step, was "Who".

But most of my memories of Cheetham Hill centre on the Cheetham Baths on Cheetham Hill Road, the Shakespeare (often referred to as the "Shakey"), the Greenhill, Premier and the Temple cinemas; St Luke's Church, Heath Street School, St Mark's Church, Smedley Hall, Alms Hill, Temple Flats and Woodlands Road Halt.

A schoolmate of mine lived in Temple Flats. On Saturday mornings he earned ample pocket money by lighting fires and doing odd jobs for the local Jewish community. Lucky him! I was sometimes fortunate to get tuppence extra to my usual Saturday tuppence for scrubbing a couple of floors and swilling our backyard.

Alms Hill was where we went jumping into the sandpits, close by Freedland's Cabinet Works. On Smedley Lane, where Kennett House now stands, was the one-time home of John Rylands, whose widow founded the celebrated John Rylands Library on Deansgate in memory of her textile merchant husband.

Heath Street School, opened on 6th October 1894, became a Central School in 1909, known as Cheetham Central School. It was there that I sat the Central Schools examination, and to this day I don't know whether I passed or not. My dad was unemployed at the time, times were hard and I never saw the letter concerning the result. A few weeks later I remember my mother saying, "You weren't really keen on going to the Central School, were you?" So I ended my schooldays at Easter 1925, aged 14, at Smedley Road Elementary School.

Woodlands Road was an unadopted, unpaved, private road, with large stumps across the road at the Smedley Lane end, barring vehicular traffic. At the side of Woodlands Road Station was a large pond where my brother and I took our fox terrier bitch to swim. We would throw a piece of wood into the middle of the pond and shout, "Fetch, Topsy!" If she didn't, we threw her in; she then got the message.

Mention the Premier, and I am reminded of a beautiful Welsh girl I "picked up" in the Theatre Royal one Saturday night, when I was "sweet sixteen". She was in domestic service (a skivvy, some people would scornfully say), at a big house, a few yards away from the Shakespeare Cinema. Poor girl, she was allowed one half day a week free, and a couple of hours to go to chapel on Sundays. We arranged to meet on her next night off, which happened to be the next Wednesday. Saturday to Wednesday dragged, but Wednesday found me spruced up and "rarin' to go" outside the Premier Picture House at 6.30pm, waiting for my "Welsh Charmer" excitedly and a little apprehensively. I need not have worried; she came, looking lovelier than on

Queens Road tramsheds - the school for tramdrivers in the 1920s

the Saturday night. I cannot recall what the film was about. Sadly, I was unable to keep our appointment for the following Tuesday, as that night found me working compulsory overtime (unpaid). Circumstances made it impossible to contact her, and I never saw the girl again; such is fate.

In the 1920s there were lots of open spaces between Lower and Higher Crumpsall. The chief landmarks were Crumpsall Workhouse, Crumpsall Hospital and Mental Institution.

In 1929 I was captain of a Timpson's team in a friendly football match against Crumpsall Mental Hospital Patients' Football Team, on their ground. It was raining heavily when we ran out on to the pitch, wearing black armbands in respectful memory of Fred Jenkins, our trainer, who had died the day before the game. When our eleven lined up for the kick-off, we were surprised, and amused, to be faced by more than twenty opponents in varied "strip"; red, blue, various striped football shirts and an assortment of pullovers. Of course, it was a pantomime game. A few of our opponents simply stood on the spot where they had started the "game", never kicking the ball but getting soaked to the skin by the torrential rain. Their ages ranged between seventeen and seventy. One old chap who stood on the penalty spot in front of our goal all afternoon beckoned me and said, "Do you know who I am?" "No, I can't bring you to mind," I tactfully replied, adding that I supposed I should. I found it hard to restrain a smile when he proudly announced, with a very serious face, "Well, I'm Dixie Dean."

By sheer accident we scored a goal, so we were immediately penalised by "our" referee for an alleged foul in the penalty area. Our goalie was ordered not to attempt to save the penalty kick. The penalty taker shot yards wide at the first attempt, so he was given a second chance, which trickled past our goalie, to loud applause from both teams. After half an hour, the whistle blew for half-time. The rain was heavier than ever, so after another ten minutes of mudlarks, time was called, and all ran off to the dressing room for a quick bath and change of clothing.

A pleasant Sunday afternoon stroll from Park View took us along Rochdale Road, past Harpurhey Cemetery, turning left into Central Avenue (Harpurhey Road), where a good panoramic view of the Irk Valley could be seen on a clear day, before descending the winding road into the valley at Waterloo Street. Then we climbed the opposite side of the valley by way of Springfield and Crescent Roads and passed the Jewish Cemetery on the right to arrive at the Italian ice cream shop on Cheetham Hill Road. Licking an ice cream cornet, we would continue our walk via Woodlands Road to Smedley Lane and turn right at the Smedley Hotel into Hendham Vale. At the spot where the Irk flows at the side of the footpath, we would throw stones at water rats before finishing our stroll alongside Queens Park.

Sometimes we would walk through the fields to Bowker Bank, a favourite haunt for the area's courting couples, returning home via Crab Lane, Blackley Village and Rochdale Road. In those days walking was an enjoyable pastime, especially on Sundays when there was nothing else to do. No cinemas, theatres, or sporting fixtures; very few people could afford a car, even at prices of £112 for a Ford or £125 for a Morris, so walking and parading in Sunday best clothes, or a "bob's worth" return by steam train to Marple were well patronised Sunday pursuits.

Errand Boy in the City

Although I must have passed the Manchester Town Hall on several occasions during my boyhood wanderings, it was not until the spring and summer of 1925 that I really became aware of the beauty of this imposing building. It was built in 1877, in the Gothic style, at a cost of £775,000, to the design of the famous architect of that period, Alfred Waterhouse.

In 1925, the building was covered by forty-eight years of industrial grime and soot; a jet black gem, creating a lasting impression on my youthful mind. It has since been cleaned to reveal its original stone colour, but whenever I read, or hear about, or even see the Town Hall, I usually visualise the "blackened Gothic pile".

After leaving school at Easter 1925 I was an office boy for six months in the shadow of the Town Hall, at Leopold Walford Ltd, a shipping office in Lloyds Bank Building, on the corner of King Street and Cross Street. They had a small coasting steamship, four or five

Manchester Town Hall

steam wagons and half a dozen horse-drawn lorries. Most of their overseas business was shipped by Manchester Liners Ltd to Canada and the USA from the then busy Manchester Docks. The steam wagons were used to carry goods to and from the Docks, while the horses and carts carried loads, mainly cotton goods, in the city centre and surrounding districts.

The job was from 9.00am to 6.00pm Monday to Friday, 9.00am to 1.00pm Saturday; wage 8/- per week. I dealt with the mail, morning and night, and the time in between was filled by running errands and delivering and collecting bills of lading between city offices and dock offices. At no time did it enter my thick skull that this was a "blind alley" job, nor that I was being used as a makeshift until the next batch of school leavers came on to the labour market after the summer holidays. I was both thankful and happy that I had any sort of job so soon after leaving school, at a time when many of my contemporaries were unemployed.

Preparing for May Day Horses' Parade in the yard of Bradford Road Gasworks

My comings and goings on my way to the warehouses, merchants' and shipping offices in Princess Street, Brazennose Street, Whitworth Street, Queen Street, Lloyd Street and other streets in the vicinity of Albert Square took me past the Town Hall several times a day. I longed to take a look inside and once ventured up the wide steps at the entrance then realising I was due back at the office, beat a rapid retreat. I had to wait 46 years before I had the opportunity to wander through the public rooms and corridors of this great landmark, when I was employed by Manchester Corporation.

Back in 1925, Albert Square looked very different from today. Smokeless zones and clean air acts were 30 years away in the future, and soot and grime had spread a sombre look over the buildings around the Square. However, it was a lively, bustling thoroughfare, with many horse-drawn vehicles, tramcars, steam wagons, a few motorcars and a lot of people, dashing about their daily business.

May Day, sometimes called "Bell Horse Day", was one of the occasions people looked forward to, because it signalled the onset of summer. Most of the cart horses were festooned with brightly coloured garlands and rosettes. The lorries of Joseph Nall Ltd, Joshua Hoyle Ltd, the brewers' drays of Boddington's, Wilson's, Chesters', Threlfall's, Kay's, Holt's, Walker and Homfray's and the Openshaw Brewery would be specially cleaned and dressed to brighten the streets as they made their deliveries. Railway carters always made a sparkling show. They spent hours of their own time grooming and decorating their horses, sometimes sleeping beside them overnight. It was lovely on May Day to see the

General Post Office, Spring Gardens

LMS, LNER and Cheshire Lines carters sitting proudly behind their charges, with the sun glistening on the polished brasses, the horses' coats glossy, the bells tinkling on the harness, as the carts made their way through Albert Square to and from the railway goods yards, city warehouses and shops.

Albert Square was the terminus for some tram routes from south and west Manchester. The numbers 11 and 12 trams trundled noisily through the Square at regular intervals as they journeyed between Cheetham Hill, Moss Side, Withington and Chorlton. They never appeared to be less than half full, and in the rush hour they were filled to capacity - "Standing room only!" as the trolley boy would shout to the large queue waiting to get home. Manchester tramcars carried millions of passengers a year and made a considerable contribution to the city rates, to the relief of ratepayers.

Many of the shops and businesses in the vicinity of Albert Square have now vanished. Facing the front of the Town Hall, between John Dalton Street and Brazennose Street, were a Post Office and Chapman's well known photography shop. This block of property hid the lovely St Mary's Church in Mulberry Street from the view of anybody passing through Albert Square. Founded in the 1790s and rebuilt in 1848, St Mary's was unseen by generations of Mancunians, except the Catholic fraternity, until a few years ago, when the obstructing property was demolished. At the Princess Street end of the Square stood a Lyons' Cafe, popular with many of the local office workers. At the Mount Street end was the Manchester School of Music (proprietor, J A Cross) which I attended for a short time in 1926. Tutors and examiners at that time included a Mr Edward Rorke, Dr Henry Reid and Basil Windsor, who for many years was Musical Director at the Manchester Hippodrome. At the top of King Street, the Reform Club was a complete enigma to me. I used to watch well-dressed men in dark suits and bowler or trilby hats going in and out of the building at all times of the day, and I was puzzled. My dad was engaged to sing at many of the political and working men's clubs in the Manchester area, so to my young mind a club was a place where people drank beer and listened to concerts. Were the well-dressed men performers? But why the daytime? Dad always went to clubs at night. I was bewildered.

One of my jobs at Leopold Walford's was to post the mail at the GPO in Spring Gardens on my way home. Built around 1884, at a cost of £120,000, this magnificent Victorian stone structure resembled a palace rather than a building of great commercial and social significance. In the cause of dubious progress it was demolished around 1970, yet another diminution of Manchester's architectural inheritance.

What a marvellous postal service we had at that time! A letter could be posted at Spring Gardens post boxes at 9.00pm and it was 99% certain to be delivered to a London or local address first delivery the following morning. I remember posting birthday cards at 8.00am on my way to work and they were delivered locally at lunchtime the same day. Postage rates were: sealed letters, 1½d; printed matter, unsealed, ½d; and postcards 1d. Rates remained static until well into the 1940s. Another important service was the "post-car" service. Apart from the four or five daily collections from district and suburban pillar boxes, there were special "post-cars" on main road tram routes into the city between 8.00pm and 9.00pm each night. One could take a letter to the nearest tram stop, wait for the "post-car" and put the letter in the post box on the platform at the driver's end. It would be safely taken to Newton Street Sorting Office for next day delivery. Saturday services were excellent and there was always a collection on Sundays.

My duties at Leopold Walford Ltd entailed visits to the docks two, three or even four times a week, and this was always an exciting experience for an adventurous 14-year-old. On my errands round and about the city I was always experimenting with new routes, discovering what to me were new streets and passages. So my trips to the Manchester Docks and Ship Canal opened up fresh fields for exploration.

On leaving the office in King Street, my walk to Deansgate to catch the 71 Salford tram was via John Dalton Street. I rarely passed the Hime & Addison music shop near the corner of St James Square without having a good look at the pianos on display. On reaching Deansgate, and turning right, I would often take notes from the noticeboard at Tyldesley & Holbrook, where football and cricket teams desiring friendly matches advertised. Sometimes I would turn left out of John Dalton Street, passing Heywood's stationers, Finnigan's departmental stores (now established at Wilmslow) and walk on to the next tram stage, thus saving a halfpenny. Doing likewise on the return journey, I could afford a penny ice cream wafer from the cart at the end of Ordsall Lane.

Variation and exploration were always in my mind, so for a change I would catch the No.30

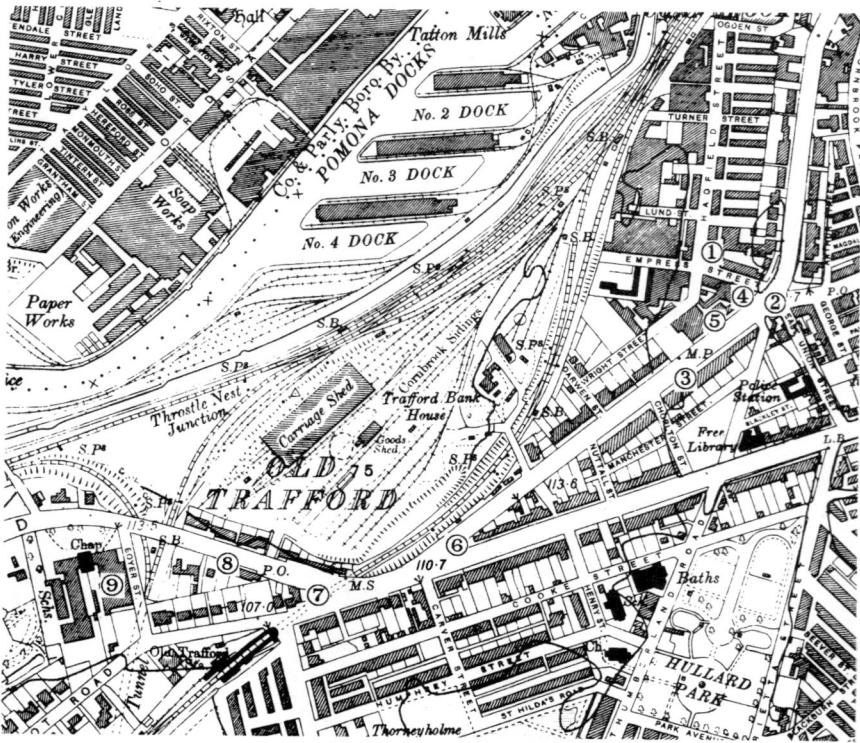

Along Chester Road: 1 Empress Brewery. 2 Northumberland Hotel. 3 Merrie Mac's. 4 Duckworth's. 5 Veno's. 6 Lavatories. 7 Burgons 8 Tramways Office. 9 Henshaw's Blind Asylum.

Manchester tram to Trafford Bridge. The route was along Deansgate, past Southern's busy timber yard at Castlefield to join Chester Road. On the left, now the site of the flyover, was French's factory, where many Hulme girls were employed. On a corner of Chester Road, facing the side of St George's Church, stood the premises of Till & Whitehead, tool and hardware suppliers. The Empress Brewery was on the corner of Empress Street, at the junction of City Road and Chester Road, and almost facing was the Northumberland Hotel, where Cecil Parkin, the popular Lancashire and England cricketer, was mine host for a number of years before his move to the Kings Head in Market Street, Droylsden. Parkin was a splendid medium pace bowler and a great entertainer. A player would roll the ball along the ground to him, he would flick it up with his toe, then catch it. When walking back to his mark to bowl, he used to let the ball run along his forearm, then knock it back to his hand with the muscle of the upper arm.

On the left, between Northumberland Road and Stretford Road, was a row of fine, big houses, which at a later date became commercial premises. About 1932 two of these houses were joined to accommodate Merrie Mac's Dancing Studios. On the opposite side of the road was a fine red Accrington brick building, Duckworth's wholesale chemist's and druggist's and next to this were the premises of Veno's, the makers of what they advertised as "Lightning Cough Cure". At the junction with Stretford Road were underground lavatories, well used by Manchester United supporters on match days. The land at the corner of Chester Road and Talbot Road was occupied by the shop of one of Manchester's best grocery firms – Burgons Ltd. A few yards past Burgons, on Chester Road, was the Manchester Tramways office, where tramcar crews changed over at the end of shifts. Next, between Boyer Street and the White City, were the gaunt, blackened and rather ugly Gothic buildings of what was then called Henshaw's Blind Asylum, later known as Henshaw's Institute for the Blind. From the top deck of the tram one could see young blind men playing a kind of football game with a ball that had a bell inside. As with piano playing, they played "by ear".

At Old Trafford in the 1920s: Sir Edwin Stockton (President, Lancashire County Cricket Club), J Sharp (Captain), H Rylance (Secretary), Macdonald, Parkin, E Tyldesley

In front of the White City the tram turned right and in a few yards, at the swing bridge over the Manchester Ship Canal, I would alight. Very often in those days the bridge was closed to traffic to allow ships to pass on their way to or from Pomona Docks. Once over the bridge it was only a short walk to the dock gates. I would make my way to the various shipping offices, from the smallest, No.6 Dock, to the largest, No.9, with its great grain elevator.

Some of my errands took me to the large factories in Trafford Park; Metropolitan Vickers (known mostly as the Westinghouse) and W T Glover Ltd, cable manufacturers. I will never forget my first visit to that great "Park". My father had told me tales about Cook's Boating Lake there, so imagine my disappointment when I didn't even find a blade of grass. "Why call it a park?" I asked myself. Years later I discovered that the land had been the country estate of the De Trafford family and the coming of the Manchester Ship Canal and Docks made it an ideal place for the development of a large industrial estate. The park gates were moved to Gorse Hill, Stretford, soon after the First World War. Ford's great motor-car works employed thousands of Manchester's workers from 1911 until 1931, when they moved to Dagenham. Some of the workforce took up their roots and moved to the new factory, but many were unable to do so. British industry was in the middle of a "slump" and the move to Dagenham was a hard blow to Trafford Park.

Boys at Henshaw's Blind Asylum playing cricket with a wicker ball containing a bell. Photographed in 1929

Strangeways

On Monday 3rd May 1926 I presented myself, clean and tidy, at the warehouse of William Timpson Ltd, 115 Great Ducie Street. I was interviewed and engaged to start as a warehouse boy at the wage of 12/- per week.

An important and significant historical event happened at midnight on the day I started my employment at William Timpson Ltd; it was the first day of the "General Strike". Walking was one of my favourite pastimes, so the fact that the tramcars were off the road was of little consequence to me. However, I was concerned about how my mother was to get to her job at Irlam's Pork Butchers in Moss Side. Cheetham Hill Road was the best bet for a lift in that direction, so we both set out at 8.00am along Queens Road, past the "Tin Tabernacle", Barney's Brick Croft and Queens Road Tram Depot. On Cheetham Hill Road a few trams were running, manned by volunteers, mainly students. Many people were on "Shanks's Pony" and nearly as many on bicycles. Very few people, or even firms, had cars in 1926.

Near Elizabeth Street my mother got a lift on a horse-drawn railway cart on its way to the Northern Railway Goods Yard, Deansgate, leaving me to make my own way on foot to Strangeways. So on I went, past the imposing Cheetham Assembly Rooms, St Chad's Church, Knowsley Hotel, turning right into Carnarvon Street, which brought me to Southall Street, where for the first time in my life I saw the grim structure of Strangeways Prison.

From the Assize Courts on Great Ducie Street it was only a few yards to Timpson's warehouse; the workers' entrance was in Julia Street. As I intended, I clocked on early that first morning and was happy to find a number of boys of my age on the warehouse staff. By the end of the week the General Strike had fizzled out. It must have been a terrible nuisance to most people, but to me it had been an exciting week. I had been involved in an event that would become a memorable occasion in British History. Things were happening for me; I was thrilled.

In the 1920s the district where I worked was quite thickly populated - mainly a Jewish community engaged in tailoring, clothing, raincoat and furniture manufacture. Great Ducie Street was a busy shopping thoroughfare, especially on Sunday mornings. There was Harry Davies's newsagency, sweets and tobacco shop, where one could get a good cup of tea for a penny. Nearby was the Jewish barber, where I often had my hair cut for 6d. At the corner of New Bridge Street I bought Fowler's meat pies for my dinner - 3d for a large wrapped pie. Then there was Black's cut price shop, where Timpson's employees bought their weekly cigarette supplies: Woodbines and Players Weights at 1/8d for 50; Players Medium, Gold Flake, Craven "A", Black Cat and Ardath (with coupons for free gifts) at 2/1d for 50.

Sabolosky, jeweller and watch repairer, would always knock a bob or two off the price of his goods if he knew you worked at Timpson's, knowing that you would recommend him to your mates. There were several tailors, "Levy's" and "Ziggy's" for instance, where we could get a suit made to measure for two to three pounds. They would always start with a price of four or five pounds, but were prepared for a bargaining price reduction.

My chief recollections of Strangeways Prison are of the mornings when an execution was taking place. On my way to the warehouse I would go down Southall Street about 8.20am and there, at the prison gates, would be a crowd reading the official notice of execution, or waiting for it to be posted up on the huge gates. I must say, that exhibition of morbid curiosity confounded me.

Quite a number of murder trials took place at the Assize Courts during the 1920s and 1930s. From the warehouse windows, on many occasions, we observed the judge in his robes arriving or departing in a large chauffeur-driven car. Criminal court cases, particularly murder trials, caused a great deal of public interest. They were a leading topic for discussion and argument in offices, factories, shops, public houses, clubs and even in the home. Full details of murder trials were reported in the newspapers, which outlined the prosecution's

A horse and cart used for Timpson's local deliveries in the 1920s

The Assize Courts, Great Ducie Street

vital evidence and defending counsel's speeches. I think the murder case that aroused most public interest between the two Great Wars was the trial of Dr Buck Ruxton.

On 29th September 1935 a human leg was found in a ravine at Moffat on the Carlisle to Edinburgh road. A thorough search at the spot revealed pieces of two human female bodies. Some pieces were wrapped in a copy of the Sunday Graphic, dated 15th September 1935, which was traced back to Lancaster. Dr Ruxton was questioned but denied all knowledge of the remains. A cleaner at his surgery found bloodstained clothing and carpets and was given a bloodstained suit and told to burn it.

Pathologists identified the two bodies as those of Mrs Ruxton and Mary Rogerson, the servant, and on 13th October 1935 Ruxton was charged with murder. Dr Ruxton's trial was in March 1936 at Manchester Assize Courts. Norman Birkett defended him to the best of his ability, but he had a hopeless task. One condemning factor amongst much incriminating evidence was the doctor's medical knowledge and surgical skill. The dismembering of the bodies was the work of an expert.

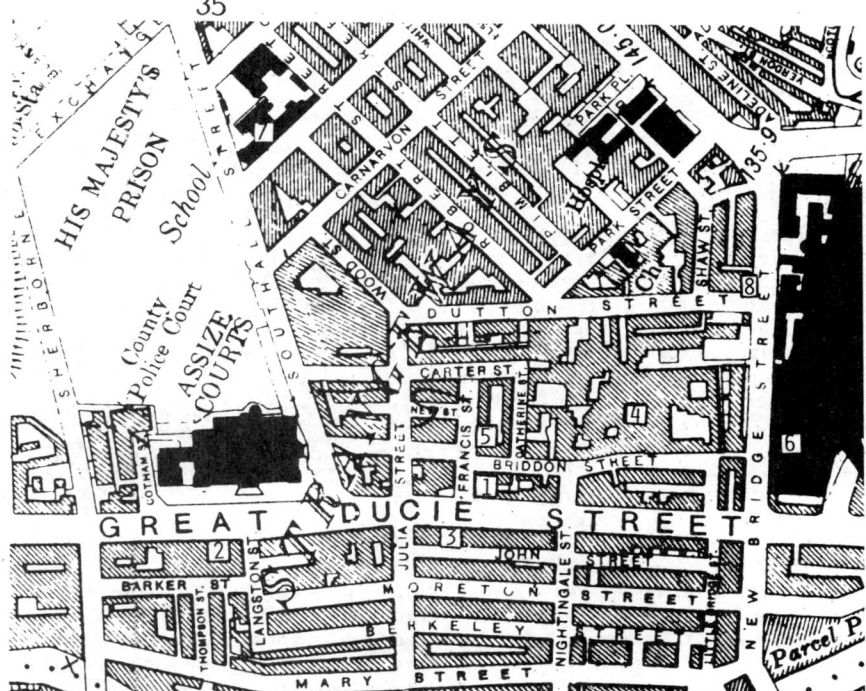

Great Ducie Street: 1 Empiric House. 2 Timpson's Warehouse (135). 3 Timpson's Warehouse (115). 4 Boddington's Brewery. 5 Salvation Army Hostel. 6 Victoria Station. 7 Southall Street School. 8 YWCA

This trial was the main topic of conversation at the time. Even in the barber's it was discussed to the exclusion of the usual subjects of football, politics and, of course, the weather. We at Timpson's were fascinated by the proceedings. We watched the jury pass on their way between their hotel and the Assize Courts, escorted by police, front and rear. We could hear them talking amongst themselves, but they were barred from talking to anyone else, hence the police escort. I believe the jurors were billeted each night while the trial lasted in the Grosvenor Hotel on Deansgate. They were confined to a room where they could have a drink and a chat before being locked up for the night in their bedrooms. It was an awesome sight each day until the trial ended; one that will never be seen again on Great Ducie Street.

Dr Buck Ruxton was hanged on 12th May 1936. The morning was dull and overcast, as it frequently was whenever an execution took place at Strangeways. Some people might sneer, saying it was typical Manchester weather, but nine times out of ten it was a fact. So much so, that on any wet, foggy or gloomy morning, local folk could be heard to remark, "Who's being hanged this morning?"

A few yards from the prison, in Francis Street, the Salvation Army Hostel was always busy with its comings and goings.

Dr Ruxton and the scene outside Strangeways Prison on the day he was hanged, 12th May 1936

Many of the released prisoners were homeless, so the first stop was Francis Street Hostel. There they could obtain a bed and a meal for a few coppers from the few shillings they got when released from prison. The hostel was a hive of activity - ambulances, Black Marias and the police were regular visitors. The Army Captain in charge must have had a troublesome time dealing with all sorts of situations. From the rear of Empiric House, which Timpson's took over in 1928, we had a grandstand view of the happenings - fighting-mad drunks being bundled into the Black Maria; unconscious and incapable alcoholics being carried into the ambulance; the police breaking up a meths-drinking party in the side street - these were everyday occurrences. On one occasion I was awed by seeing one of the staff laying out a corpse in one of the dormitories. Police searching for crime suspects made regular visits, many of which were fruitful. However, not all the men who used the hostel were layabouts. A few could be seen leaving for work in the mornings and returning for a meal and bed each night.

When I was 17, for a dare with a workmate, we went into the hostel for our dinner. We tried to disguise ourselves by dirtying our faces, ruffling our hair and putting on dirty, worn-out shoes. A large plate of stew cost 2d. We sat at a bare wooden table to eat our food, amid a motley collection of humanity. As I took my first taste of the stew, I overheard one scruffy individual remark,

Cockshoots, Great Ducie Street

"Bloody strangers in the camp" and the man facing me, who had no dinner in front of him, was staring at me with longing eyes, which put me off my food. The stew smelled greasy; my appetite vanished, so I pushed my plate across to the hungry looking chap who had never taken his eyes off me. He rapidly scoffed that greasy stew - a clean plate in about two minutes flat.

It was a revolting sight to witness the meths drinkers passing the bottle round, mouth to mouth, without ever wiping it. Then to watch them become stupid and glassy-eyed filled me with disgust. If you got too near to them, the stink was obnoxious. The police and ambulancemen hated the job of collecting them and would avoid the ordeal if possible.

Anyhow, we were assured of one glorious smell at least once a week, when the splendid aroma of malt and hops pervaded the Strangeways air from brewing day at Boddington's.

On a short walk to St Mary's Gate in 1926, leaving Timpson's by the staff entrance in Julia Street and turning right into Great Ducie Street, we would pass a shop where a pleasant young girl named Mary used to serve us with Brookes's cream cookies at 1d each, and they were delicious. At the corner of Nightingale Street was the Continental Trimming Company, and on the opposite corner was Levine's, the tailors. Next door but one was the Strangeways Post Office; then at the corner of New Bridge Street, the Ducie Hotel, with Cockshoot's car showrooms, offices, and repair garages on the opposite corner - a well known name in the early days of the motor car. Then followed tailors' material and haberdashery shops, and a public house, before one came to the railway bridges connecting Victoria and Exchange Stations.

A glance over the railings near the Exchange Station approach brought into view the steps and landing-stage used by the old Irwell pleasure steamers. The small wooden shed at the top of the steps, in my time a newsagent's and tobacconist's kiosk, was in earlier years the booking office for the boat trips. Thomas Cook's had a single storey travel agency office near to the corner of Victoria Bridge Street. At the corner of Deansgate and Victoria Bridge Street stood the Grosvenor Hotel, and a few yards further on the right hand side of Deansgate was yet another fairly large residential hotel, the Deansgate, which was destroyed by a disastrous fire in the 1940s. Wagstaff's piano and organ shop was on the corner of Deansgate and St Mary's Gate.

Manchester Cathedral and the old landing stage at the turn of the century

Timpson's

William Timpson Ltd had two warehouses: 115 and 135 Great Ducie Street. Men's, youths' and boys' footwear was stocked at 135; ladies' and children's at 115. Neither building was purpose built, both being converted shop properties. The Ladies' Warehouse, as we called it, was the larger. Originally it must have been about six large shops with living accommodation and it was a maze of dark narrow passages, small stockrooms and creaking fixtures and floors. Work was hard for us boys under such conditions. Carrying loads of shoes and sundries from the various departments to the packing room, or climbing fixtures to get out orders for the 120 shops from 8.30am to 6.00pm Monday to Friday, 8.30am to 1.00pm on Saturdays was tiring. And it was all for 10/- or 12/- a week. Nevertheless, we had lots of fun.

Like most factories and warehouses we had our share of characters, always good for a laugh or a chat. Caramel Earnshaw, not long out of school, was so nicknamed because he was constantly sucking caramels. Every day he spent his dinner money on sweets - I think he had a good meal when he got home from work. He never ailed, although I can't remember the condition of his teeth. The lads taunted him with questions such as, "What are you having for dinner today, Devon Cream or Rum and Butter?"

There was George Belfield with his military obsessions. Short haircut, waxed military moustache; he marched about with a

The Boys' Refuge, later Empiric House, with the Salvation Army Men's Hostel at the rear

perfectly straight back. He certainly looked the part of a regular soldier of that period. However, it was rumoured that his army service had not taken him any further than Heaton Park, where he had broken a leg in training before being discharged. His bearing was so impressive that I never believed the story. He was a humorist who delighted in telling, with a serious face, stories of his exploits at the battle of Tellhertokeepit during the African Wars, when they fought man-eating natives with bladders on sticks. He used to have the new boys spellbound - until they got wise to him - with tales about his pets: a fantailed rabbit and a white blackbird!

Another character was Hughie Williams, the packer-cum-boilerman and maintenance man. I would think he had had little education and read even less. He had a reputation for mispronunciation. I think it started when he told somebody that he had bought a Portugal (portable) gramophone and a monogamy (mahogany) table. I once heard him say, "I've got to check the fire distinguishers today."

By 1928 the Timpson warehouses were too small. The firm was expanding at the rate of about eight new shops a year and it was essential to find more storage space. Fortunately, there was a vacant building on the opposite side of the road, almost facing number 115. The Boys' Refuge had been built in the 1890s to accommodate "problem boys", but after the First World War it was used by the Ministry of Pensions. Timpson's bought this building and converted it into what was considered to be, at that time, a "modern warehouse". The new warehouse, "Empiric House", was the new home for ladies' and children's footwear, offices and the sundries department. The flitting took place during Bank Holiday Week, August 1928. As the old solid-tyred Thorneycroft lorry moved the goods from number 115, a new lorry transferred the men's and boys' section from 135 to 115. The empty 135 was taken over by the shop fittings department. Empiric House, aptly named after a brand of Timpson's shoes, was a four storey building with basement, offices and packing room on the ground floor, and provided adequate stockroom for a few more years.

The staff was given a "pep talk". No expense had been spared to make Empiric House into an up-to-date distribution centre, so we were told. To enable the new system to reach

Empiric House and the extension on Great Ducie Street (the repairs factory) which was built in the early 1930s

maximum efficiency, new work disciplines had to be adhered to. On a fixed day each week, all floors **must** be red raddled and polished. All fixtures and stock **must** be dusted, and stocks replenished from reserves. A pleasant staff canteen had been installed. All this, we were told, was for **our** benefit, would make our daily tasks much easier, and we should be justly proud. At that time, Timpson's were extremely lucky in having a very loyal, hard-working young staff, but it soon became obvious that hard work and enthusiasm could not possibly cope with the expected work load. In less than a month there were signs that the floors and fixtures were being neglected, and with the approach of the Christmas trade rush, the polishing and dusting was abandoned completely. It was realised that the weekly supplies to 130 retail branches up and down the country were more essential than polished floors that one could eat meals off. In fact, more young lads had to be employed in an endeavour to get goods away to a tight schedule.

The work was really hard, the action fast, "at the double" all day and every day. There was no time to get bored (a word rarely heard in those days) at Timpson's; in retrospect I think it helped to develop a sense of humour peculiar to Timpson's staff in those years, and the fact that something was always happening helped us to get the job done in the quickest time. If the packing room hadn't completed the day's schedule by normal finishing time, the entire warehouse staff had to stay until the packing cases were being loaded on to the transport ready for a quick getaway the following morning. There was no payment for overtime and it was galling to have to work until 7.00pm or 7.30pm, waiting for the whistle signalling that the packing room had completed the day's orders. A mad stampede to the locker room followed, and we would wend our weary way homeward with tired limbs and aching feet. The warehouse manager's lame excuse was that it would be unfair to the packers if he allowed the remainder of the warehouse staff to go home when they had finished the day's orders. However, if he calculated the work would require at least two hours' overtime for completion, he would arrange for a fifteen minutes' break at 5.00pm, when a cup of tea and a cake would be provided. There never appeared to be enough cakes to go round, which resulted in a frantic rush to the canteen. One had to be sharp off the mark, or else one would be an "also ran". To be fair, I do not think the directors of the firm knew very much of what went on after 5.30pm.

In an effort to make an extra shilling or two, the lads collected waste rope and string from the unpacking department to sell to a Jewish chap in Mary Street. He would pay 2/6d for a large carton of waste rope and 4/- for a carton of string, according to weight. Sometimes, after weighing, he would say he could only pay 2/- and 3/- a carton. It often took months to collect a carton of waste, so the boys didn't take too kindly to the reduction. So what we did, before taking the waste for weighing, was to lift about half out of the carton, pour a few pints of water on to the waste at the bottom and replace the dry stuff. This added a few pounds to the weight. All went well on the first occasion and I think we were paid a few coppers more than usual. But it must have roused the Jew's suspicions. The next time, he felt right down to the bottom and declared, "You've wet that rope. I'll give you 1/6d; take it or leave it."

We didn't have morning or afternoon tea breaks in those days, but we were not completely deprived of sustenance as a girl came round with a tray selling cakes, chocolates and sweets. It could be both daunting and tempting on days before pay day, feeling hungry, with only a penny in one's pocket for tram fare home. Many a time I spent my last penny on a bun, ate it in three or four bites and then regretted it all the weary way home. Was it worth it, as I dragged my tired, aching limbs through Cheetham and along Queens Road? This may have subconsciously developed a kind of grudge in my mind which prompted me to play a trick on the canteen. Of course, as usual, it was a huge joke to me, but taken rather seriously by the canteen manageress.

I cut some brown soap into small chunks, wrapped them in Devon Cream toffee papers, put them into a paper bag, then slipped the bag on to the girl's tray when she wasn't looking. What I imagined was somebody buying the toffees and putting the soap in his mouth to suck, ha, ha, ha! That did happen, but the man dashed to the canteen manageress, demanding his penny back. She had a "platonic" friendship going with

115 Great Ducie Street, Timpson's Men's Warehouse, after the Manchester Blitz of May 1941. Only a few pairs of shoes in the sample room survived. Stock, sales records and orders were destroyed

the warehouse manager and reported the matter to him. The impression was that it was a device for stealing a pennyworth of sweets. "Gus" (sometimes "The Ghoul"), the warehouse manager, was simply furious when his ladylove told him, and as usual threatened the culprit with the sack, if he could be found. With my reputation for fun and games, I knew it was inevitable I would be questioned, so I was prepared and denied any knowledge of the affair. For the umpteenth time I had escaped being sacked, and I remained a loyal, hard-working member of the firm for thirty-five years.

Lewis's in 1926

Piccadilly and Market Street

By the 1920s the Portland Street end of Piccadilly was the home of the Reference Library and the Henry Watson Music Library, which I joined at the age of 14 to borrow the works of the great composers. On the opposite corner, facing Newton Street, was one of Manchester's best hotels, the Queens. Between Newton Street and Lever Street, in the middle of a row of shops and offices, No.55 was the Manchester Corporation Transport offices. A large oak-fronted shop on the corner of Lever Street, Dunn & Co, sold the best quality men's hats in Manchester. Warehouses lined Parker Street where the bus station, Piccadilly Plaza and Sunley Buildings now stand. The warehouses were destroyed by enemy action during the last war.

At the end of Mosley Street, in a triangular block of shops and offices facing the gardens, was the Tramways Parcels Depot, and a few doors away was a wallpaper shop, where I frequently bought cheap decorating materials. On the corner of Oldham Street was the jewellery business of Saqui & Lawrence, where my girlfriend and wife to be bought me a gold wristlet watch for my 21st birthday present. A few yards away on the site that became Littlewood's store stood the Piccadilly Picture House, which had a ballroom in the basement. I well remember attending a Melody Maker Dance Band Contest there in 1927, won by a ten-piece band from Oldham, the "Black Bandits".

A little nearer to Tib Street the well lit "State Cafe" was the fashionable place to wine and dine in those days, and on the corner of Mosley Street and Market Street the good old Irish Linen Shop displayed its first class goods. At the corner of Lewis's Arcade was Wiles, Manchester's famous toy shop, which attracted thousands of children and parents at Christmas time.

At night, high on the wall above the Parcels Depot overlooking Piccadilly, the mutagraph flashed news items in electric lights between the advertisements. Many tramcars passed through Piccadilly and there always seemed to be lots of people about, even at night; it certainly was a lively place.

Lewis's Arcade was the notorious stamping ground for the "fairies", or "ladies of easy virtue". They appeared to start their beat from the Arcade, before parading singly along Market Street, then turning into Fountain Street, York Street and Mosley Street, to return to Lewis's Arcade if they had not

Piccadilly

picked up a client. Sometimes they made a brief visit to the Shakespeare Hotel or the old York Hotel in search of business.

It was in Fountain Street where I had my first encounter with a "fairy", and I was scared speechless. I was 16 at the time and recently breeched into my first long trousers (boys didn't wear long trousers until they had left school). The "fairy" looked old enough to be my mother, or maybe grandmother. She deliberately tried to bar my way, at the same time greeting me with the words, "Are you looking for a good time, Jack?" My reaction was swift and silent. With my best body swerve, I evaded any contact and was yards past in a flash, with the "fairy's" embarrassing insults spurring me on my way. "Do you want your nappy changing?" she shouted, as I turned into Market Street. I was simply furious, but never gave a thought to retaliate. My aim was to get away as fast as possible.

Market Street was the busiest and most congested street in the city and had been for nearly a hundred years. A nineteenth century historian wrote: "Market Street in the old town, perhaps the most congested street in Europe." No attempt at a regular pattern of street planning occurred until 1930. The road junctions were controlled by point duty policemen outside the Queens Hotel, Oldham Street, occasionally High Street, Cross Street and Deansgate. The Cross Street/Corporation Street/ Market Street crossing, busiest in the city, was considered to be the most difficult point duty job in Manchester. Some of those point duty policemen, by their gestures in beckoning the traffic, became well known characters.

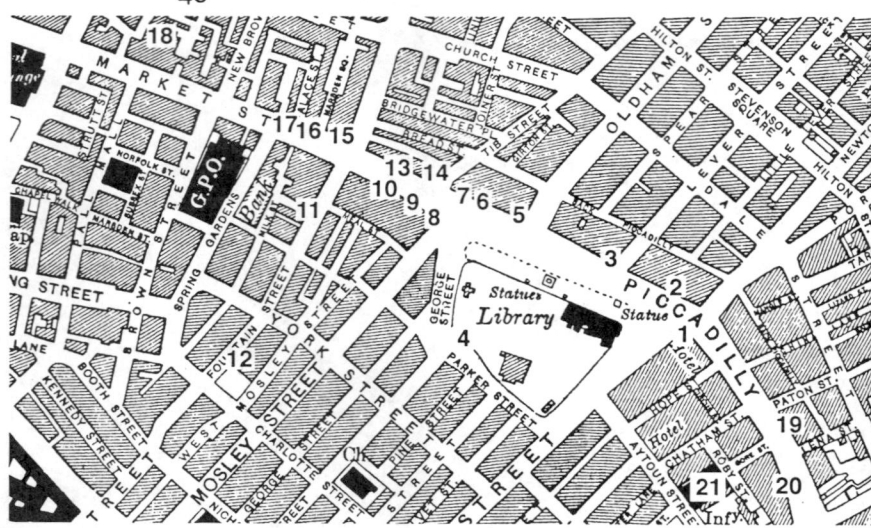

Market Street and Piccadilly: 1 Queens Hotel. 2 Manchester Transport Offices. 3 Dunn & Co. 4 Parcels Depot. 5 Saqui & Lawrence. 6 Piccadilly Cinema. 7 State Cafe. 8 Irish Linen Shop. 9 Wiles' Toy Shop. 10 Lewis's. 11 Shakespeare Hotel. 12 Garrick Hotel. 13 Hill's Tripe Shop. 14 Ryland's Warehouse. 15 Hope Brothers. 16 Henry's Stores. 17 Market Street Picture House and Yates's Wine Lodge. 18 Harry Liston's Bar. 19 Rofe's Sports Shop. 20 Hobbies Ltd. 21 Roby Street Hospital.

Lewis's was the busiest and most popular department store in the town. In the days before Christmas it would be packed to suffocation; at times it was almost impossible to get in through the doors. Queues of parents with children extended along Fountain Street in the direction of York Street, waiting their turn to deliver their requests to a jolly old Father Christmas. On the top floor was a popular restaurant and ballroom. Jack McCormack's Orchestra played light music in the restaurant during the afternoon, making an afternoon tea of strawberry jam and scones really enjoyable. I well remember "shaking a leg" at private dances up there.

Sometimes, when I had 3d to spare, probably saved out of my dinner money, I would call in to the Shakespeare, York or the Garrick for a quick gill of mild before dashing for the tram and home. I think the beer was a halfpenny dearer at the Garrick, it being a rather exclusive "men only" pub.

In the early 1920s, between Tib Street and High Street, was a sooty black block of warehouses, offices and shops fronting Market Street. In the middle of the row was Hill's UCP tripe shop, with a cafe upstairs where I remember eating the most delectable steak puddings. A few years later the site was occupied by the splendid new Rylands building. At night, a searchlight swivelled in an arc from the roof of the new block, piercing the dark Manchester skies. I never knew the exact reason for that, but it was said at the time that it directed aeroplanes to Barton Aerodrome.

On the corner of High Street was Hope Brothers, a good class men's wear and sports shop, and a few yards away on Market Street was Henry's Stores, a second-rate Lewis's. The thriving Yates's Wine Lodge occupied the corner of Pool Street and opposite was Manchester's most popular coffee house, the Kardomah. Between Brown Street and Corporation Street a narrow passage led into Cannon Street, and along here was the lively Harry Liston's Bar, well known for lunchtime concerts.

Both sides of Piccadilly between Newton Street and Ducie Street had interesting shops - none more so, to me, than Rofe's sports goods shop, where I once bought a cricket bat. On the other side of the street was Hobbies Limited, with their window display of toy steam engines and clockwork trains.

Traffic congestion - Police on point duty, corner Market Street and Cross Street, in 1928

Theatreland

To my mind, the Peter Street/Oxford Street area of Manchester was probably the most exciting part of the city, evoking many happy memories of people, places and experiences. Theatreland, from Whitworth Street to Quay Street, consisted of four "live" theatres and seven cinemas, some of which had interludes featuring live artists. Manchester Hippodrome at the corner of Oxford Street and Great Bridgewater Street was my favourite theatre, where my dad introduced me to the world of entertainment at the age of four. However, the first venture on my own was to the old Tivoli, known affectionately as the "Tiv".

In between films in 1922 the "Tiv" had interludes of live entertainment, mostly singers. Friday night was "go as you please" talent contest night. I well remember the happy occasion when I was ordered to go and support my dad, who had entered the talent contest. He was a vocalist in a trio, at that time trying to establish a reputation, who sang to piano accompaniment. They did reasonably well in taking third prize. Twelve turns were entered and given three minutes each to do their act. Six of the turns managed to complete their allotted time, but the remainder were forced to make premature exits, some after thirty seconds only. If the audience did not like a turn, or sometimes even if they did, they could give turns the "bird", or "screaming Richard" as my dad sometimes preferred to call it. The "bird" would start with a few people stamping their feet and whistling. Others would gradually join in until the din became deafening. Giving the "bird" appeared to be great fun for the audience, but to me it was a pitiful sight which saddened me.

It was the custom for theatres and cinemas to display their weekly programmes in shop windows, giving shopkeepers free complimentary passes for the privilege, and I was fortunate in having a regular supply of free passes from the shop where my mother worked. One such picture house was the Futurist, situated between the Albert Hall and Deansgate. It was a purpose-built cinema, smaller than the Theatre Royal and Tivoli (converted theatres) and I remember seeing some of the early Charlie Chaplin and Buster Keaton films in that cosy cinema. It closed during the 1920s to become one of the first car showrooms in the city.

There was a period when I was given a free pass for the Gaiety almost every week (yet another converted theatre) and this was my favourite city centre picture house. The "silent" films at the Gaiety were not silent by any means. They were accompanied with appropriate "programme" music by the excellent orchestra led by the local favourite, Louis Blatnor, and there was always an interlude of variety. A lovely singer named Dorothy Penny was often featured, being a particular favourite with the Gaiety regulars. It was said that the "Dorothy Bag" was named after this charming young lady by her father, William Penny of Stockport, the maker of that dainty evening bag. Whenever I hear or play the romantic waltz song, "What'll I Do?", I am reminded of Dorothy and the Gaiety, where I first heard the haunting melody. I cannot remember any of the films; my interest was concentrated either on the orchestra or the interlude artists. Performances were con-

1933 advertisement

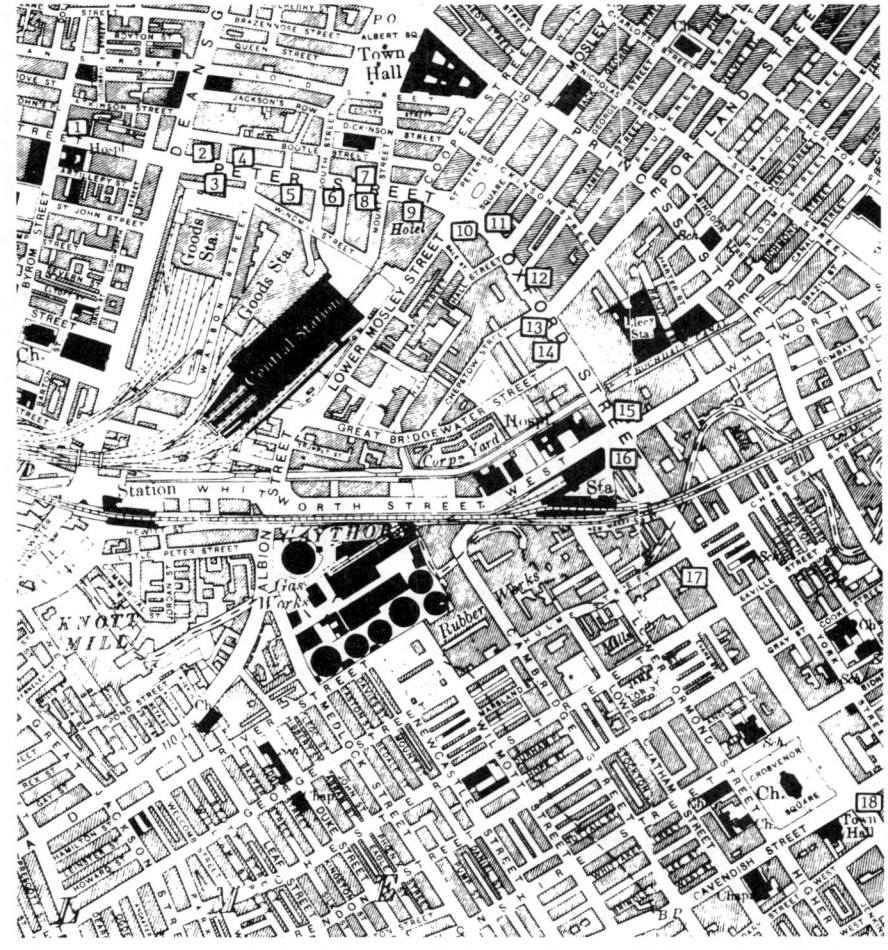

Peter Street and Oxford Street: 1 Opera House. 2 Futurist Cinema. 3 Tivoli. 4 Albert Hall. 5 Free Trade Hall. 6 Theatre Royal. 7 Gaiety. 8 YMCA. 9 Midland Hotel. 10 Prince's Theatre. 11 Paramount Cinema. 12 Plaza Dance Hall. 13 New Oxford Cinema. 14 Manchester Hippodrome. 15 Palace Theatre. 16 Tatler Cinema 17 Regal Cinema. 18 Grosvenor Cinema

tinuous from 1.00pm to about 11.00pm and I can remember times, during school holidays, when I went into the Gaiety about 1.30pm and came out about 9.00pm.

My first visit to the grand old Theatre Royal was in 1922, when my father passed on to me a ticket which had been given to him by somebody who was unable to use it. Once again, my visit was made memorable by the musical interlude between films; an excellent baritone singer. One of his songs, another first for me, was "My Little Grey Home in the West", which remains one of my favourites to this day. A film I do remember seeing at the Theatre Royal was "Syncopation", featuring a "silver tone" tenor called Morton Downey. This was my first "talkie" and to this day I can hear and imagine Morton Downey singing "I'll Always be in Love with You", the principal number in the film.

I will never forget one particular New Year's Eve. Dave, my pal, had "chatted up" a girl where he worked and arranged to take her out on New Year's Eve. She wouldn't agree unless she could take her friend along, so Dave arranged a "blind date" for me. We all met at the Cenotaph, and my enthusiasm for a good night out rapidly dwindled. Dave had told me, maybe kidded me, that the girl he had invited was a "smasher", and he believed my blind date was even better. True, his girl was a chic, bonny lass, but mine, poor thing, looked dowdy and old-fashioned. New Year's Eve, and she wore a straw hat with ribbon round, long skirts and, worst of all, button-up boots.

Short skirts above the knee and art silk stockings with high heeled shoes were the fashion for smart young ladies. "What a pity! She's a very nice girl, really," I said to myself as we walked to the Theatre Royal.

Disappointed, and a little embarrassed, I was as amiable as possible; after all, it was New Year's Eve. During the course of the evening I discovered that she was the youngest of a large family and lived in a small terraced house in the "Hanky Park" district of Salford. She was fifteen years of age and learning to be a machinist in the "rag trade" at a wage of 8/- a week, which she had to tip up to her mother. In those days it was quite common practice, when a child grew out of clothing, to hand it down to the younger children to wear out. I think the clothes and footwear the poor girl wore, which had gone out of fashion in the early 1920s, had belonged to her mother. I was from a poor background, but this to my mind was real poverty.

In St Peter's Square was the music shop and theatre booking

Portland Street

agency of J A Cross, the proprietor of the Manchester School of Music in Albert Square. A few yards away was Dingley's high class florists and fruiterers. Then at the corner of Oxford Street was Boots the Chemists, who were open all night for urgent prescriptions. Close by, on Oxford Street, was the newly built "posh" cinema, the Paramount, in later years known as the Odeon. Wadsworth's, the organ builders, and the Plaza Dance Hall were the last notable buildings before Portland Street.

Portland Street was lined end to end with warehouses, mainly textile, with a row of small shops and three pubs between Charlotte Street and Princess Street. The properties on this row had stone steps, protected by iron railings outside, leading down to the cellars. Two of the public houses were adjoining and the other was next door but one. The Circus Tavern has the smallest bar I have ever seen. The pub is a converted house with a small hallway where a bar, no more than a yard wide, has been made on the left. What was the parlour of the house is the "bar parlour", and the living room has become the "snug".

By far the largest warehouse in the street was that of S & J Watts, one of Manchester's more attractive buildings. They employed a large staff and were reckoned to be a good firm to work for insomuch as any vacancies attracted many applicants.

At the corner of Mosley Street and Princess Street is the splendid Manchester Art Gallery

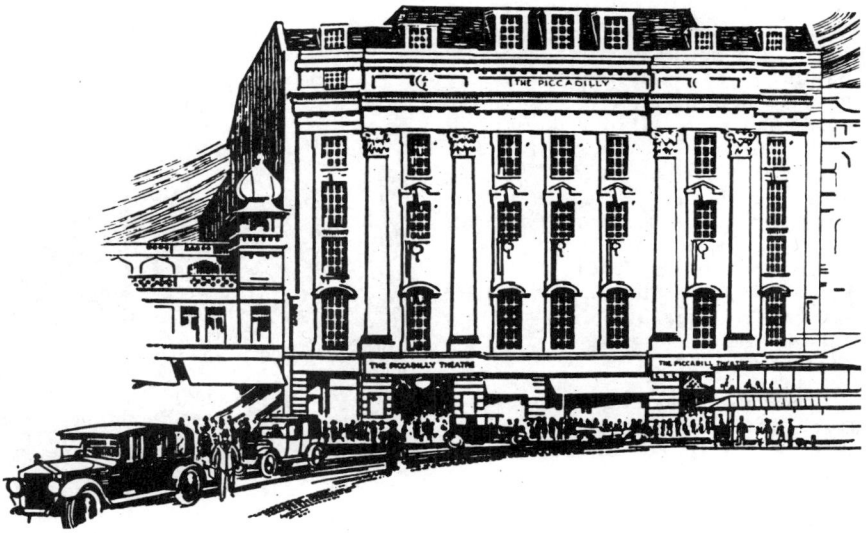

Piccadilly Theatre

and at the rear of the Art Gallery, on Princess Street, is the glorious Italian Renaissance architecture of the Athenaeum. My most vivid recollection of the Athenaeum concerns the feeling of elation when playing for a "select dance" at such an exclusive club. However, enthusiasm was somewhat dampened at the interval when we could not find a bar, so we had to make a dash to the Seven Oaks Hotel in Nicholas Street to recharge our batteries to cope with the rigours of the second half.

Opposite the Plaza on Oxford Street, near to the corner of Lower Mosley Street, was the well-loved Prince's Theatre, the home of musical comedy for many years. I never had the pleasure of seeing inside the Prince's, but I well remember my mother telling me what a comfortable and elegant theatre it was. It was there she had been enthralled with such shows as "Chu Chin Chow" and Captain Fraser-Simson's "Maid of the Mountains" with the marvellous José Collins.

On the corner of Chepstow Street was a Lyons' Teashop and next door was the Oxford Street Picture House, the venue in 1928 of the first "talkie" in Manchester - "Uncle Tom's Cabin". A sweets and tobacconist's shop separated the Oxford Picture House from the Manchester Hippodrome. To my mind it was a better theatre than the Palace or the Opera House. From the age of 12 until the closure I enjoyed its many variety shows, revues and even periodic water spectaculars. A good seat in the balcony with an unrestricted view of the stage (no pillars) cost only 6d.

Among my favourite artists I saw there were: G H Elliott, "the chocolate coloured coon"; Billy Bennett; Norman Evans in his sketch, "Over the Garden Wall"; Layton and Johnstone, a superb double act who sang songs at the piano; comedian Harry Tate with his motor car and golf sketches; Billy Russell, the English working man, dressed like a navvy, and Albert Whelan, with his beautifully spoken monologues. One of the first turns I saw - it must have been just after the 1914-18 War - was Harry Weldon, billed as "Stiffy the Goalkeeper". He performed in football gear, between goalposts, jumping, diving, prancing about and picking an imaginary ball out of the back of the net.

I must not forget the ladies, such as Nellie Wallace, Lily

Oxford Street and Palace Theatre

Morris (comediennes), Hetty King and Ella Shields (male impersonators) - all top line variety artistes between the wars. Then there were the great bands; Jack Hylton's, Harry Roy's, Billy Cotton's, Hot Club of France with Django Reinhardt and Stephane Grappelli, and Bert Ambrose's Band. Novelty acts, such as Wilson, Kepple and Betty, eccentric dancers; Bennett and Williams, with their one-string fiddles; Arthur Prince, ventriloquist, were always a feature in variety shows at the good old Manchester Hip.

I remember seeing the local flyweight boxing champion of the world, Jackie Brown, at the peak of his career, coming out of my favourite theatre. As he came down the steps at the front of the theatre with his wife he waved and smiled at the crowd of admiring fans. He wore a "Teddy Bear" coat, and his wife was adorned in a beautiful full length fur coat, with expensive jewellery.

Next to the Hippodrome was the splendid building of the well known textile firm of Tootal Broadhurst & Lee, facing the grand facade of the Calico Printers' Association building on the opposite side of Oxford Street, where horse-drawn carts laden with large bundles of materials could be seen coming and going from the loading bays. People who had jobs at either of those two great commercial houses were much envied. It was said that they had steady, secure jobs for life.

At the Whitworth Street end of the row was the Palace Theatre and Bars, yet another place with happy memories for me. The Palace, opened in 1891,

St Peter's Square and Midland Hotel before the library was built

mostly staged musical comedies and top class revues such as C B Cochran's shows. Seats were dearer than the Hip, the cheapest, in the gallery, costing 1/-. That was really good value for such fine shows as "The Desert Song", "Rose Marie", "Hit the Deck" and many other great musicals featuring star performers of the day, like Elizabeth Welch, Jack Buchanan and Jack Hulbert. During the 1930s the Palace introduced more variety seasons, usually during the summer months. The great artists I remember seeing include such names as Gracie Fields ("Our Gracie"); George Formby (Junior, of course); the Two Leslies (Sarony and Holmes); Western Brothers, Mrs Jack Hylton's Band with Alex Templeton, the blind pianist, composer of "Mr Bach Goes to Town"; Florrie Ford; Dorothy Ward; Les Companions de la Chanson, the superb French singers who made the lovely song "Little Jimmy Brown" their signature tune, and many others.

One stupendous performer I will never forget was the fabulous tenor saxophone player Coleman Hawkins. He wasn't a showman, oh no!, but what a musician - the likes of whom I hadn't previously heard. I will never forget the way he nervously ambled on to the stage, wearing a plum coloured suit and light brown boots, clutching his instrument with obvious affection and playing a straight chorus of "Honeysuckle Rose", followed by chorus after chorus of rhythmic extemporisations. I had never heard anything like it and I was spellbound.

Diagonally opposite the Palace, near to the Oxford Road Station Approach, the Tatler Cinema had a continuous programme of newsreels and cartoons throughout the afternoons and evenings. It had a reputation as a haven for drunks, a cosy place where they could "sleep it off".

To my mind, the gallery seats in the Opera House, Quay Street, were the worst of any theatre in Manchester. They were not separate seats, simply numbered spaces on long forms. I well remember my disappointment on my first visit there at the age of 14 to see the opera "Carmen". The cheapest seat was 2/-. I took jam jars back to the Meadow Dairy on Rochdale Road and beer and Guinness bottles to the Queens Arms at the corner of Queens Road and Topley Street to get the 2/1d. (The 1d was needed for tram fare; ½d each way from Queens Road to High Street.) I enjoyed the opera, but was bitterly disappointed with the theatre. "Two bob for a seat like that!" I said to myself. "Not a patch on the Manchester Hippodrome." Nevertheless, I did the very same thing next time the Opera

1933 - the new library under construction

Company came to town, to enable me to see "La Boheme".

Public houses and bars in the vicinity of theatreland were well patronised in the evenings. The Oxford Hotel, facing the Palace, near to Jimmy Reno's musical instrument shop, was usually full of theatregoers and theatrical people, and so was Tommy Duck's at the back of the Prince's Theatre. I never visited the Prince's Bars, almost opposite the Prince's Theatre, because they had a reputation for being a "Nancy boys" rendezvous. One could certainly see life in that part of the city in those days!

In the 1920s, Peter Street and St Peter's Square looked very different from today. Facing the Midland Hotel, between Mount Street and St Peter's Square, was a sombre looking block of shops and offices. The new Cenotaph, in memory of Manchester's 1914-18 War dead, had been erected on the site of the old St Peter's Church. The wonderful new Central Library, the best example of classical architecture built in Manchester during the past fifty years, was opened by King George V on 17th July 1934. The foundation stone of the new Library was laid by Prime Minister James Ramsay MacDonald on 6th May 1930. I thought the old Reference and Henry Watson Music Library in Piccadilly was a wonderful place, but the new Central Library was magnificent. I have spent happy hours delving amongst the music scores and literature.

In 1926 I was unemployed for a couple of weeks so I joined a class of out of work boys at the Manchester YMCA in Peter Street. I chose shorthand and office procedures. Classes were held in the afternoons, between 2.00pm and 4.00pm. Then we were free to use the facilities of the gymnasium and swimming bath. That was terrific! There was an indoor running track on a balcony along the sides of the gymnasium, and it was lovely to run thirty or forty laps, followed by a refreshing bath and a few lengths swim in the plunge. Fortunately, or unfortunately, I found a job during the second week, so I didn't learn much shorthand, but the recreation was marvellous.

Deansgate

Deansgate in the 1920s was an extremely busy thoroughfare; the main road to the Docks and Trafford Park, where thousands of people were employed. It was also a main road from the farmlands of Cheshire to the Manchester markets, and from the East Lancashire mills and Rossendale Valley in the north came great quantities of cotton goods and footwear. Transport of all kinds, horse-drawn vans and lorries, steam wagons, motor vehicles, even handcarts, slowly but surely wended their way in both directions. The junctions at Blackfriars Street, John Dalton Street, Peter Street and Liverpool Road were controlled by point duty policemen who had a difficult job regulating the flow of traffic.

The city end of Deansgate was renowned for its fashionable shops and departmental stores. Kendal Milne's occupied large premises on both sides of the road. King Street, St Ann's Square and Street were lined with stylish, expensive shops, patronised mainly by a wealthy clientele from such places as Altrincham, Bowdon, Hale Barns, Didsbury, Chorlton-cum-Hardy and Bramhall.

Starting from the point where Victoria Street and Deansgate joined, where Oliver Cromwell's monument looked up Deansgate watching for the approach of the Royalist forces, one would pass the Deansgate Hotel on the right and Wagstaff's piano and music shop on the left, then beyond Blackfriars Street was Thomas Armstrong's opticians. Facing the fascinating Victorian Barton Arcade was the Deansgate Picture House, which reminds me of a rather frightening experience in my young life. I was about 16 years old and, along with five or six young chaps from the warehouse, went to see a film called "The Dangers of Ignorance". There were separate performances for males and females throughout the week. It was a "horror film", insofar as it illustrated venereal diseases at all stages, and the consequences when risking casual sexual intercourse. There was a grave risk of going blind, deaf, daft or even of dying. It certainly put the wind up me, completely putting me off associating with girls for at least a month.

A few yards from the Deansgate Picture House was the Houldsworth Hall, the scene of the popular lunchtime concerts. My pal Dave lived there; his parents were caretakers. At the rear of this block was Parsonage Gardens, where the local warehouse and office workers enjoyed the summer sunshine and air during their lunch hour. In the Parsonage was Ormes' Billiard Hall, where professional billiards matches were regularly staged. Snooker didn't become popular until the late 1930s. I remember following the fortunes of the great billiards exponents of the day, such as Willie Smith, Walter

The Cromwell Monument

Lindrum, Tom Newman, Walter Donaldson and Inman in the "Stop Press" of the Manchester Evening News, especially when they played at Ormes. Willie Smith was my favourite; I have no idea why, except that he always seemed to win.

Three well known establishments between King Street West and Bridge Street, still there to this day, were Waring & Gillow, high class furnishings; the Halifax Building Society and Forsyth's music shop, yet another shop I couldn't pass without looking in the windows. Just past John Dalton Street was Heywood's, Manchester's leading stationers, and the good class departmental stores of Finnigan's. The building between Queen Street and Jackson's Row contained the offices of the Manchester Education Committee and on the opposite side of Deansgate were the Inland Revenue offices. At the corner of Quay Street were the shop and showrooms of Cranes, the piano dealers, still another place I could never pass without envious glances at the lovely pianos I could not afford. A few yards further along Deansgate was the Milton Hall, where I remember attending a Manchester. School of Music students' concert in 1925.

At the Deansgate end of Liverpool Road stood the City Exhibition Hall, a Victorian iron and glass construction, well used, but then looking rather tatty. In 1932, arrangements to build a new exhibition hall were made, but never matured. I was always fascinated by the small stalls on the narrow balcony, which we called "Mugs Alley". It was interesting to watch the demonstrations of household - mainly kitchen - gadgets, easy, time-saving utensils that worked splendidly in the hands of the trained demonstrator, but in the home, without skilful operation, were soon discarded as useless.

Opposite the City Hall, on Liverpool Road, was Lord's, a place where one could buy camping and hiking equipment at reasonable prices. I bought a tent there for 12/6d, which gave excellent service and many hours of pleasure to me and my pals.

At that time the most impressive building on Deansgate in my opinion was the gothic architecture of Rylands' Library. Though it was less than forty years old it was then as black as the hobs of hell. In 1892 Mrs John Rylands bought the magnificent library of Earl Spencer of Althorp and to house it the building in Deansgate was erected as a memorial to her husband.

St John Street, street of surgeons and medical specialists, always fascinated me with its Georgian architecture and charm. Whenever I passed that way I visualised grand gentlemen wearing top hats and frock-tail coats, accompanied by beautiful, fashionably dressed ladies, alighting from hansom cabs and entering their lovely town houses.

I have many happy memories associated with that part of

Deansgate: 1 Deansgate Cinema. 2 Houldsworth Hall. 3 Kendal Milne's. 4 Cromwell Monument. 5 Wagstaff's music shop. 6 Waring & Gillow. 7 Forsyth's. 8 Halifax Building Society. 9 Heywood's. 10 Finnigan's. 11 Manchester Education Offices. 12 Cranes music shop. 13 Milton Hall. 14 Tyldesley & Holbrook. 15 Nags Head. 16 Rylands Library. 17 City Hall. 18 Lord's.

Deansgate, looking towards the Cathedral

the city, mostly in connection with my hobby as a dance band pianist; pleasurable functions at the Squirrel Cafe facing the Houldsworth Hall, Wood Street Mission, the Nags Head Hotel in Jackson's Row, Manchester Limited Restaurant in the Royal Exchange Arcade, and at the Caxton Hall, near the Flat Iron Market on Chapel Street, Salford.

Although it was as long ago as 1928, the Caxton Hall function is as vivid in my mind as if it had occurred last week. The occasion was a dance to wind up a Communist Party Rally.

(During the 1920s and 1930s the Communist Party had far more supporters throughout Britain than it has today.) The band consisted of five youths of understandably limited experience, and at the end of the evening we were somewhat embarrassed by the request for "The Red Flag", instead of the usual National Anthem. We hadn't previously given it a thought, so were quite unprepared. At such times it usually falls on the pianist to rescue the situation, and this was no exception. The band lads looked in my direction, so I struck a chord and hoped for the best. Lo and behold, the crowd burst into song with "The Red Flag", which to my relief I recognised as the tune of "Maryland". We fumbled our way through it, and all was well.

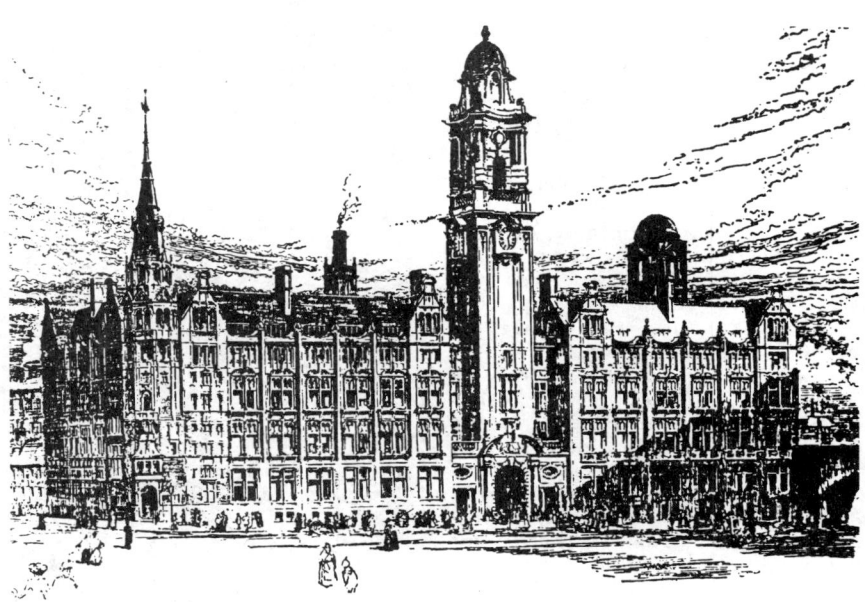

The Refuge building

Oxford Road and Stretford Road

Oxford Road and Stretford Road were busy shopping thoroughfares in the years between the two Great Wars. Both roads were flanked by hundreds of terraced houses in the then thickly populated districts of Chorlton-on-Medlock, Hulme and Greenheys.

Between Whitworth Street and the railway bridge was the grand building of the Refuge Assurance Company with its impressive clock tower. To secure a job at the Refuge was the ambition of many Central and Grammar School leavers, it being considered a cut above the many textile offices. Underneath the railway bridge was, according to the sign above the window, a surgical appliance shop, but I don't think the appliances they sold were used by surgeons. I never saw anyone come out with a wooden leg, or surgical corset. Next came Gaskell's Turkish, mineral and swimming baths, before reaching Charles Street. On the next block was Mamelok's well known musical instruments shop, with their teaching studios and showrooms. Next door was Watts' Brothers, theatrical costumiers and agents, and almost facing were the newspaper premises of the Daily Herald; the Regal Cinema was later built alongside them.

Where the Mancunian Way crosses Oxford Road stood the Clarendon Hotel, a red and white glazed brick building renowned for its concert room. There were still some fine shops on both sides of the road as far as Brunswick Street, but trade was diminishing and the bulk of shopping was rapidly being transferred to Stretford Road. Oxford Road and Rumford Street were notorious for "ladies of easy virtue"; frequently the butt of comedians' jokes at the local theatres.

All Saints Church and graveyard stood at the corner of Oxford Road and Cavendish Street, a prominent Manchester landmark. Here the tramcars turned right to approach Stretford Road on their way to Old Trafford, Moss Side, Chorlton-cum-Hardy, Stretford, Sale and Altrincham. Opposite the church, on the corner of Grosvenor Street, was the Grosvenor Picture House, where I saw the early "talkie" film, "Sunny Side Up", featuring Janet Gaynor and Charles Farrell - a delightful romantic picture. Snuggling up to my girl friend on the back row, I was enthralled by the novel experience of romantic talk coming from the screen.

Facing All Saints Church in Cavendish Street was Chorlton-on-Medlock Town Hall. Built in 1830, a relic of the days when Chorlton-on-Medlock had its own Council, it was still in use for social functions. I have fond memories of playing there for private dances.

Back on Oxford Road, a few yards past the Grosvenor Cinema was the Oxford Bar, then a few yards down Rusholme Road was Grimshaw's popular

All Saints in the 1890s

dancing academy. At the corner of Booth Street West stood a large branch of the Manchester & Salford Co-operative Society and on the opposite side of the road, the La Scala, a new picture house built in the 1920s.

On the corner of Brunswick Street stood the College Hotel. This was the terminus for the No.51 tramcars, where the trolley boy would take the trolley-pole round to the opposite end of the tram while the driver changed ends. Then off it would go down Brunswick Street on its way to the other terminus at Miller Street, facing the Ducie Bridge Hotel. The tram passed the Ardwick Empire Theatre (next door, facing Ardwick Green, was the Coliseum Picture House), then went down Chancery Lane, Pin Mill Brow, past Ancoats Hall into Ancoats Lane, into Swan Street and Miller Street.

My earliest recollections of the Royal Infirmary take me back to 1915, when I went with my mother to visit my sick dad. He had just undergone what was then a serious operation on his kidneys. Two large stones, like big marbles, were removed and I remember them being kept in cotton wool in a tin box in a dresser drawer for many years. I also attended the Royal Eye Hospital in Nelson Street many times during the following two or three years. Mother and I would arrive at the hospital at 9.00am and frequently did not get away until late afternoon. Naturally, at my age, I found those periodic visits terribly boring. But my patience was usually rewarded on the way home by a visit to Paulden's or Lewis's for tea, toast and cakes. Failing that, it would be a call at Marks and Spencer's Penny Bazaar, to be treated to a lead toy soldier to add to my collection. Of course, the war was on, so they were always in khaki uniform.

On the corner of Denmark Road was the Rivoli Dance Hall, where Nat Gonnella played in the band in the late 1920s. A few yards away was Bill Swan's piano showrooms, where in 1935 I bought (on the never-never) a new Kessels baby grand piano for £59, at £1 per month. To obtain the order Mr Swan brought me from Droylsden to his shop, made the deal, arranged terms to suit me and then took me back to Droylsden. Such enterprise deserves success!

At the Rusholme end of the Royal Infirmary, on High Street (Hathersage Road), were Victoria Baths, the best swimming baths in the town and the

Oxford Road: 1 Refuge Assurance Building. 2 Gaskell's. 3 Mamelok's. 4 Daily Herald. 5 The Clarendon Hotel. 6 All Saints Church. 7 Grosvenor Picture House. 8 Chorlton-upon-Medlock Town Hall. 9 Grimshaw's. 10 Manchester & Salford Co-op. 11 La Scala Cinema. 12 College Hotel. 13 Burlington Cafe. 14 Church of Holy Name. 15 Royal Eye Hospital. 16 Paulden's. 17 Rivoli Dance Hall. 18 The Rusholme Repertory Theatre.

home of the South Manchester Swimming Club. It was a 33-yards plunge, whereas most others were 25 yards, and some only 20 yards. South Manchester was one of the leading clubs in the North of England. Between the wars, I visited these baths on many occasions as a spectator, and occasionally to have a swim. Living in Harpurhey and Blackley, I was a staunch Harpurhey supporter and frequently watched their water polo matches with local rivals at the High Street Baths.

At the corner of Great Western Street, on the site once occupied by the Manchester Carriage Company (forerunner of Manchester Corporation Transport) was the Rusholme Repertory Theatre. Then, almost facing Dickenson Road, stood the Trocadero Cinema, affectionately known as the "Troc". The "Cass", or Casino, to give it the full title, a picture house with a ballroom attached, faced the Birch Villa Hotel, and next to the hotel, almost opposite Platt Lane, was a favourite little theatre of mine and many other people's - Harry Leslie's Pavilion. Concert parties and pier shows from the various seaside resorts visited Harry Leslie's during the autumn and winter months and were very popular. There was usually a pantomime at Christmas. I spent many happy hours being entertained in that little theatre.

On Friday nights and Saturday afternoons Stretford Road was alive with shoppers buying in for the weekend or looking for bargains. Paulden's store on the corner of Stretford Road and Cambridge Street was second only to Lewis's in popularity. A few yards away was a territorial drill hall, and in the row opposite there were at least two shoe shops, Stead & Simpson and William Timpson. A friend of mine from

Timpson's warehouse was directed to that particular branch as a relief assistant for the pre-Whitsun rush trade. The Saturdays before Whit Sunday were the busiest in the year, when shop assistants were rushed off their feet from nine o'clock in the morning to ten or eleven o'clock at night. My pal was late in arriving at Stretford Road and dived into the first shoe shop he came across. He apologised for being late to the girl assistant, who told him the manager was in the back storeroom. So he hung up his raincoat and started to acquaint himself with the stock. About ten minutes later the manager appeared on the scene and enquired what my pal was looking for, and who he was. It turned out that my chum had gone into Stead & Simpson in his haste, which called for a further apology before he sheepishly crawled away to make more apologies to the Timpson manager, who had by then given him up as lost or absent.

A little further along the road was Winifred's Dancing Studios. Winifred was the daughter of the "Welsh Wizard", Billy Meredith, the Manchester United, Manchester City and Wales footballer. Woolworth's had one of their "nothing over the price of sixpence" stores at the corner of Great Jackson Street. Between Upper Jackson Street and Chorlton Road was the Zion Institute, opened as a school on 1st October 1875; it has a special place in my memory because it was there that I played my first gig at the age of 14. The function was a wedding reception, for which I was paid 5/-. The other three members of the band were in their twenties, and I remember my mother putting in a brief appearance to check the kind of company I was associating with in the band. Finally, at the corner of Chorlton Road was Kershaw's, a large, prosperous greengrocery shop.

Oxford Road and the Church of the Holy Name in 1928

Ancoats

Ancoats Hall, then known as the Horsfall Museum, stood at the junction of Ancoats Lane and Every Street, with a fairly large garden in front. The museum closed in 1955; the building was then used as a Railwaymen's Club and was later demolished.

A few yards along Every Street was the University Settlement, affectionately known as the "Roundhouse" because of its shape. It was a recreational centre with educational facilities. Dances were a regular feature, much appreciated and enjoyed by many of the local people in this thickly populated district. One of the founders of this nineteenth century "leisure centre" was Herbert Philips of the well known Manchester firm, J & N Philips.

A little further along Every Street towards All Souls Church, Tutbury Street slopes down to Palmerston Street, facing Ardwick Lads' Club, where I played for dancing regularly on Wednesday nights for six years. Mr Noel Timpson of William Timpson Ltd, the shoe firm which started life in Oldham Street, was the chief patron and supporter of the club.

At the Ashton New Road end of Every Street was Every Street Elementary School, one of Manchester's first schools resulting from the Elementary Education Act of 1870. The school was opened on 8th January 1874. Not far from Every Street School was Russell Street, where my dad's partner in a double act lived; my father used to pull my leg by saying he had been down "Every Street in Manchester". My most vivid memory of Russell Street relates to Teddy Hyams, a first class drummer who also lived there. Teddy, eventually a professional with the Billy Ternant Orchestra, was giving a few lessons to Alf White, the drummer in our band. Alf owed me 10/- from our Friday night job, so he asked me to call to see him at Teddy's home on the Saturday lunchtime, after work. Alf's lesson ended, and the three of us had a real good "chin wag". Alf was delighted with a pair of maracas Teddy had sold him, and after a short demonstration he put them down on a chair. We carried on chatting and then suddenly Teddy's four years old son burst on to the scene, gleefully shouting, "Look what I've found, Daddy!" We looked, and the front doorstep and footpath were covered in what looked like dried peas. He had smashed the maracas on the doorstep. I'll never forget poor Alf's face; he was nearly in tears. He had paid 12/6d for them only a fortnight beforehand. Teddy had already spent the money and was stony-broke, so poor Alf had to stand the loss with sympathetic apologies.

On the opposite corner of Ashton New Road to the Mitchell Arms, where the River Medlock flows under the road on its way to Philips Park, stood the local "flea pit", the Don Cinema. At the rear, in Cambrian Street, was a church school which I think belonged to St Mary's in Hillkirk Street, near to Pat Dowd's mineral water works. The schoolroom in Cambrian Street had been built early in the nineteenth century. "Where are we playing next Saturday?" Charlie the saxophone player would say. "At Charlie Dickens's place," (meaning Cambrian Street School) our drummer would reply. At each end of the room was a brightly burning coal fire surrounded by an iron fireguard. The bare wooden floor was rough tongue-and-groove with protruding knots and nails - certainly not an ideal dance floor! Lavatories were outside in the school yard; not a pleasant experience on a bitter cold winter's night. The piano had had years and years of hammering; it was out of tune, with several notes missing. When the man in charge came into the room Charlie would loudly proclaim, "Here comes Mr Squeers!" Such was the Dickensian character of the place.

Butler Street was a lively thoroughfare with many shops, public houses and a cotton mill. A regular tram service (No.25) went to and fro between Stevenson Square and the Bradford Road/Hulme Hall Lane terminus. My uncle Tom and auntie Louie Cornforth had a grocery shop near to the Bradford Road end and just round the corner on Bradford Road was Bannerman's large mill. Another large mill in Ancoats where some of my relations worked was McConnel's, on the

Ancoats: 1 Ancoats Hall. 2 Roundhouse. 3 All Souls' Church. 4 Ardwick Lads' Club. 5 Every Street School. 6 Don Cinema. 7 McConnel's Mill. 8 Wesley Hall. 9 Hetherington's. 10 **Ancoats Hospital**

side of the canal off Ancoats Lane.

Between Heyrod Street and Adair Street was Wesley Hall and facing, on the Lane and along Pollard Street, was the large engineering works of Hetherington's. That was one of the works where apprentices, on finishing their "time" and becoming entitled to "full money" (about 30/- a week) would be sacked - quite a common occurrence in engineering works in those days.

Other notable landmarks in the densely populated area of Ancoats were New Islington Baths (one of Manchester's first swimming baths), Ancoats Hospital, Stony Brow, New Islington Public Hall, Boardman's Brewery, Tame Street Lodging House and St Michael's Church. St Michael's was renowned for the beautiful tableaux of the Italian community in the Whit Friday processions and they were always the last church procession to leave Albert Square.

New Islington Baths was what today would be called "basic", but to me it was a good 33 yards swimming bath. My father

The "Roundhouse", Every Street, c1900

told me that Mayfield Baths, near London Road Station, was even older. New Islington Public Hall was a typical nineteenth century assembly hall, where my dad promoted dances, and at a later date I had the pleasure of playing for dancing.

Stony Brow, off Store Street, was recognised as the steepest incline of any street in Manchester. When I was about 13 years old, as a dare, I ran up and down Stony Brow four times without stopping. I finished, puffing and blowing, but put on a brave face by sprinting the rest of the way to London Road Station. However, I was glad to find a seat on the train to Marple. Happy days!

Midday fog in Piccadilly, 1932

Victoria Station to St Ann's Square

Any mention of Victoria Station reminds me of several incidents connected with this old terminus of the Lancashire & Yorkshire Railway and its surroundings. I have vivid memories of September 1939, seeing lines of evacuees, mostly children, wending their way along Great Ducie Street, Victoria Street, New Bridge Street, Corporation Street and Hunts Bank. Some were chatting gleefully in anticipation of an extra holiday, others strolling, sad faced, feeling homesick and abandoned, even before they had boarded the train.

Earlier that year I attended the old Manchester Grammar School building, then being used as a recruiting office, to try to join the Barrage Balloon Squadron. Although I had always played football and cricket under the handicap of very poor eyesight, I was curious to know whether I would be accepted as a volunteer. The three mates I went with were called up for service on the Friday before war was declared; I was rejected.

Facing the Long Millgate entrance to Victoria Station, until quite recently, was the Manchester Arms Hotel, the one time house of the Haworth family, a name which appears in the church register back in 1699. During the 1930s I sometimes called there for a "quick un" on my way home from work. It was like stepping back into history at least a hundred years. I don't think the furnishings or decoration had been changed since Queen Victoria came to the throne. The solid oak doors, bar and chairs, and the dark green painted walls, although terribly dingy, always fascinated me. I would leave by the back door which, strange as it might seem, was in Corporation Street.

I remember once coming out of the Manchester Arms into a dense Manchester fog. Very few Manchester inhabitants under the age of 40 can have the remotest idea of what a real Manchester "pea souper" was like. Bumping into people, lamp posts, walls and railings; wheezing, panting and gasping for breath were hazards to be encountered on several days during the winter months before 1955, or thereabouts. As I emerged on to Corporation Street, I almost collided with a man tentatively trying to cross the road, so I escorted him safely into Balloon Street. Remarking about the filthy weather, I asked where he was bound for. "Stevenson Square," the stranger replied. "So am I," I said. "Follow me then," remarked the man, at which I was a little taken aback. He had a stout stick in his right hand, and it was then I suddenly realised he was blind. Apart from the discomfort of breathing, the thick fog was no handicap to him. He led me up Balloon Street, across Shudehill, up Thomas Street and across Oldham Street into Stevenson Square without incident, in less than half the time it would have taken me.

A few doors away from the Manchester Arms on Long Millgate was Carr's, where I bought bone meal, lime, basic slag and grass seed for my garden. At the corner of Hanover Street, facing the station wall, was the Bay Horse, another of Manchester's old public houses now demolished.

In the late 1920s a private coach firm, Tognarelli's, ran a regular service from near the Poets Corner site to Bolton, and it was a very good service. I think the fare was 1/- return. Another excellent private bus service between the wars was run by Mayne's of Clayton, between Dale Street and Kershaw Lane, Audenshaw.

From Hunts Bank to Fennel Street, on Victoria Street, was a row of shops and offices – Palatine Buildings – which at one time had been the site of the Palatine Hotel, one of Manchester's leading hotels. There was a large furniture shop, a sweets and tobacconist's, and at the Fennel Street end was what the Timpson's chaps called the "Dirty Book Shop". The books on display could today be seen for sale at any church jumble sale – how times change!

Early this century, the area surrounding the Cathedral was a hive of industry and commerce. In Victoria Bridge Street, on the banks of the Irwell, was the old established druggist firm of James Woolley's, who started business back in 1844. Fennel Street and Hanging

Ditch were lined with cheese stores and grocery warehouses. In the middle of Hanging Ditch, facing the back of the Cathedral, was the Hanging Ditch Post Office, a busy office in this lively part of the city. At the Cateaton Street end of Hanging Ditch stood the Corn Exchange, a grimy but noble building and on the Fennel Street corner was the Exchange Hotel, one of the city's smaller commercial hotels. The Crown & Anchor in Cateaton Street, very busy at lunchtimes and in the evenings was a calling shop for a "quick un" - a glass of 3d mild beer. On pay night it might run to a glass of Worthington "E" (4½d) at the Mitre Hotel, Cathedral Yard.

One of my favourite haunts was the old Market Place area of the city. The area had changed very little since Victoria Street had been made up in 1837 and Corporation Street built in 1845. Except for a few hawkers' handcarts and a few shops, all signs of the market had long since disappeared. But it was a boozers' paradise - a relic of the past importance of the market and its traders. During the late 1920s and 1930s I visited all the public houses in the area, some more frequently than others. These visits were usually in the form of a "quick un" on my way home after chasing about the warehouse all day.

Birthdays, weddings, engagements and stag nights always provided a good excuse for a

The Slip Inn

night on the town. We usually started with a round or two at the Old Millgate, a Tetley's house in the Market Place. Then perhaps one in the Falstaff, London Bar, Shambles (Wellington), Blue Boar, Bulls Head or the Coronation, without leaving the Market Place. Maybe we would finish up with a plate of shrimps or oysters in Sinclair's Oyster Bar. People partook of Guinness and oysters at Sinclairs to get themselves into what they called "fine fettle". At that time I didn't realise what they were getting in fettle for.

In addition to the above there was the Fox on Victoria Street; Mitre and Crown & Anchor near the Cathedral; Victoria on the corner of Victoria Street and Deansgate, and the Grosvenor on the corner of Deansgate and Victoria Bridge Street, all within a stone's throw of one another. One was certainly spoilt for choice in this old part of town.

Another popular hostelry was the Slip Inn, known by most people simply as the Slip, where in days gone by Leslie Stuart was resident pianist. At the turn of the century it was the best known music hall concert room in Manchester. Amongst the famous stage performers who appeared there were Wilkie Bard, Whit Cunliffe and Fred Barnes, the idol of the ladies.

On Corporation Street, where Marks & Spencer's store now stands, was the tobacconist's shop of Major Drapkin, the manufacturer of Gem and Critic cigarettes, quite popular brands in those days. On the opposite side of the street was Sefton's Bar, with mainly a lunchtime trade.

Parker's Restaurant on St Mary's Gate, between the Royal Exchange and Deansgate, was a favourite place to dine or hold functions. They had a resident small orchestra playing light music during the afternoons and evenings.

The LONDON AND MANCHESTER OYSTER COMPANY, LIMITED

SINCLAIRS.

Noted for Whitstable Oysters, Lobsters, Crabs.

Sandwiches, Salads, &c.

VICTORIA STREET.

Draught and Bottled Bass and Worthington's Ales.

Truman's London Stout.

Guinness's Harp Stout.

Wines & Cigars.

In Exchange Arcade, under the Royal Exchange from Cross Street to St Ann's Square, was the sheet music shop of Wright Greaves Ltd, where I spent pounds of my hard earned money. But it was money well spent - even today, nearly sixty years on, I derive great pleasure from those copies which cost me 6d or 1/- each.

On the corner of Bank Street and St Ann's Square was a very busy Post Office and between Bank Street and St Ann's Street stood the old established wines and spirits merchants, Marks Ltd.

Facing the old Cross Street Chapel, at the side of Willoughby's Restaurant and Bar, a narrow footway led to St Ann's Church. At the side of the Church, another narrow passage led into King Street, then Manchester's high class shopping street. The small garden in front of the Church was, like the Parsonage Gardens off Deansgate, an oasis of peace and quiet from the turmoil of the city traffic.

Oldham Street

Looking at the blighted Oldham Street of today, few people under the age of fifty realize that between the two Great Wars it was one of Manchester's premier shopping streets. Apart from having two large departmental stores of high repute, Affleck & Brown's and Lomas's, Oldham Street was lined end to end with fine shops. Between Thomas Street and Whittle Street was William Timpson's shoe shop, the first of the countrywide chain, opened by the firm's founder in 1865.

On the opposite side of the street was Howard's piano and music shop, and a few yards away Marks & Spencer's Penny Bazaar. At the corner of Thomas Street was the English Leather Company shoe shop, next door to the Kings Hotel. Then came Yates's Teetotal Tavern, a favourite place for a cheap lunchtime snack. As a young working lad with little money to spend, I found this place a God-send. I would almost run there from Great Ducie Street, all uphill, to enjoy a large home-baked barmcake with cheese (1½d) and a cup of tea (1d). The cheese was beautiful, mature red Cheddar, unlike the tasteless stuff sold as cheese today. The tea was not as good as the food, however; it had that peculiar taste of most tea urn brews.

About the year 1930 there were at least half a dozen tailors' shops in Oldham Street. Burton's had two shops, then there was the Fifty Shilling Tailors where I bought my first dress suit (dinner jacket), which lasted me twenty hardwearing years. The cost was three guineas, including a pair of patent cloth dance shoes. At the corner of Dale Street was Weaver to Wearer Ltd, where a man's made-to-measure suit could be bought for as little as 35/-. I remember buying a suit there - one of their better cloths, mind you - for 45/-. As with Kendal Milne's, if you told your friends or neighbours that you had bought something at Affleck & Brown's they gazed at you with envious eyes.

The mother of one of my boyhood playmates had rooms above one of the shops on Oldham Street. She was in business as a palmist, under the name of Madame Vera, and numbered among her many clients were businessmen, councillors and even detectives, so it was said.

Nearby was the Prince of Wales Club on Lever Street, where the bookmaking fraternity gathered for leisure and business matters. The husband of a cousin of mine was a regular frequenter of the club; so much so that he often forgot to go home for his dinner. My cousin prepared a hot meal every day, and one day her patience was exhausted. So she put his dinner in a basin, tied it in a red handkerchief and set off hotfoot for the Prince of Wales Club. Her husband was there all right, boozing and oblivious to the fact that he had been expected home two hours ago. Hiding the dinner basin behind her back she marched up to him and said, "Do you intend coming home for your dinner?" Before the bewildered bookie, sitting among his cronies, had time to answer, Peggy plonked the dinner in front of him, shouting, "Don't bother! There's your bloody dinner! I hope it chokes you!" After such a "showing up", I understand his punctuality improved, and little wonder.

Before Woolworth's moved to the newly-built store on the corner of Piccadilly, they occupied premises adjoining Yates's Wine Lodge. When that place was vacated it became a fun fair, with amusement stalls and freak shows reminiscent of the Golden Mile at Blackpool. One such event that caused quite a stir in the city was the fasting record attempt by a man who went under the name of Sacco. People paid an admission fee to watch poor Sacco go steadily "down the nick". It never ceases to amaze me what some folk find amusing. Needless to say, I never saw the poor soul, I just followed the

Oldham Street

daily reports in the Manchester Evening News. At the time the word "Sacco" found its way into English language, when people referred to anybody thin and weedy.

The public houses in Oldham Street were the Albert at the corner of Whittle Street, the Castle Hotel, almost opposite, the top Kings and the bottom Kings. Then there were the Yates's Wine Lodges at the corner of Great Ancoats Street and next door to Woolworth's at the Piccadilly end of the street.

The Castle Hotel was the best for evening entertainment. On Friday and Saturday nights they had paid artists, and at other times it was what was called "free and easy". Anyone was free to give a song, or perform their "party piece". So after a few drinks to get him in the mood, a customer would ask the poor suffering pianist to play "Danny Boy", "Sweet Adeline", "Nellie Dean" or "Moonlight and Roses", so that he could "do a song", as he put it. "Why not?" the pianist would say, then, probably under his breath, "Yes, let 'em all suffer!" But there were times when some of the volunteers turned out to be fine singers or really good entertainers.

Yates's Wine Lodges were favourite for shoppers calling for a "quick un", mainly women; and for topers who did not want music or any entertainment to distract them from "solid supping". The floors and tables were bare wood, sawdust covered the floors and there were no one-armed bandits. Playing of games was not encouraged, in fact they provided nothing that would entice people to linger, other than good wines and beers at a cheap price.

Stevenson Square was the "Speakers' Corner" of Manchester on Sunday afternoons and nights. There would be several meetings going on at the same time, mainly religious and political, with a few social and pressure groups now and again. The humorists and entertainers, usually local politicians, attracted most people with their funny stories and witty quips in reply to the hecklers. Of course, in those days there was no Sunday football, cricket, tennis, bowls, theatre or cinema entertainment, so weather permitting, the "tub thumpers" of Stevenson Square drew large audiences, and those meetings were good for the Sunday trade in the nearby pubs.

Church Street was a street of warehouses and one hotel, the Unicorn. To me, the Unicorn was the best place in town for draught Guinness, Bass and Worthington. On the opposite side of the street, extending to Tib Street, was the large warehouse of one of the best known names in Manchester, J & N Philips. In my younger days this company was considered to be one of the best employers in the city. Perhaps not in the same league as the CWS, Balloon Street, or the Refuge Assurance, or even S & J Watts - or William Timpson - but they had a very good reputation. As with most of the warehouses at that time, recruitment was mainly of school leavers and steady employment was assured if a youngster was conscientious, eager to learn the business and kept his nose clean.

The Britannia Hotel in Newton Street had a popular concert room several nights a week. Also at the Great Ancoats Street end, the Lord Nelson did good business with local workers, especially with those from the Newton Street Sorting Office. Near to Hilton Street is the Kensington Hotel, then with a green and cream tiled frontage, and at the corner of Dale Street was Harry's Bar. This was a small, single room pub, mainly dependent on a passing trade of regular drinkers of its well kept Tetley ales. I don't think it was "men only", but I never saw a woman in there.

South Manchester

During the late twenties and early thirties, footballing, gigging and courting acquainted me with the neighbourhoods of Greenheys, Moss Side, Whalley Range, Withington and Chorlton and their many landmarks. I well remember, when going to play football at the YMCA Sports Ground, the open fields on both sides of Princess Road after passing the Princess Road Tram Depot. The building of the Manchester Corporation Withington Housing Estate had just started, the road had been widened and the tramcars ran along a reservation in the centre of the road. Beyond the YMCA were Hulme Grammar School Playing Fields, followed by more open fields before arriving at what we called the Aerodrome (Hough End Playing Fields), Manchester's first airfield before Barton came into use. Between Nell Lane and Barlow Moor Road is the enormous Southern Cemetery, reputed to be the largest in Britain, the final resting place of the airman Alcock, who with his partner Brown made the first non-stop crossing of the Atlantic in 1919.

I still have happy memories of playing football on what I and many more youngsters considered to be the best parks pitches in Manchester - Christie's Playing Fields on the opposite side of Barlow Moor Road.

From Barlow Moor Road it was only a short walk to the Mersey banks, much frequented by courting couples during summer nights. I have fond recollections of strolling by the riverside to the Easter Fair at Northenden, to join the crowds on the big swing-boats, "dobby horses" and coconut shy, or enjoy a drink at Jackson's Boat.

Terraced houses lined both sides of Greenheys Lane from Burlington Street to the junction with Denmark Road. At this point, above the Co-op shop, was one of the district's

Political meeting in Stevenson Square

popular dance halls, the Rialto. Then on the corner of Denmark Road and Princess Road stood the old building of the Palatine Bottling Company, facing the Alexandra Hotel on the corner of Moss Lane. Between Moss Lane East and Raby Street was one of the local cinemas, the Royal and just round the corner, where Raby Street meets Moss Lane East, stood the Princess Picture House, where I frequently went with a complimentary pass. Princess Road Elementary School, between Raby Street and Great Western Street, boasted two pupils who became famous names in their chosen careers. Isobel Baillie, the universally known opera, concert and recording soprano, in her later years an eminent teacher of singing, received her basic education at the school and Don Welsh, the England international footballer, was also a pupil at Princess Road School. As a boy he was football crazy and spent most of his spare time kicking a "tanner ponk" about in the back entry in Bickley Street, Moss Side.

The subject of football reminds me that Charlie Moore, right full back of Manchester United in the 1920s, who partnered the great Jack Silcock, was for many years following his retirement from the game landlord of the "Little Western" pub at the Whalley Range end of Great Western Street.

Probably the best known dance hall in the area was Cowan's on the corner of Bickley Street and Raby Street. It was very popular as a teaching academy. My sister-in-law was on the staff there for twelve years and Albert Cowan, the owner, was a prominent member of the National Board of Dancing Adjudicators, travelling up and down the country judging dancing competitions and contests.

I could never understand why the hotel at the corner of Moss Lane West and Alexandra Road was called the Prince of Wales, and the hotel on the corner of Moss Lane East and Princess Road was the Alexandra. The reverse order always seemed more logical to me.

Further along Moss Lane West is Hyde's Anvil Brewery, where on brewing days one could enjoy the aroma of hops and malt. On the opposite side of the road, above the Co-op, was Merrie Mac's Dancing Studios, where I enjoyed many Friday nights with several of my chums with whom I worked. We took part in all the dances except the tango. I don't know what it was we disliked about

Manchester Aerodrome, Alexandra Park, 1922

the tango, but when the dance was announced the four of us would dash to the door, ask for a "pass-out" and head for the pub across the street. The "Tango Exodus" caught on rapidly with the young men, but it really riled the girls! Girls were barred from having a "pass-out", so they were left to suffer tango instruction and practice without male partners. When we returned to the room, half an hour and two pints later, we were always greeted with ironical cheers, and who could blame them?

On summer days I found great pleasure in such simple and cheap pursuits as walking, swimming at Broadfield Road Baths, a game of tennis in Alexandra Park or listening to the band in the park. Afterwards there was an enjoyable glass of dandelion and burdock at Womack's, the herbalist's on Princess Road, or a Walls ice cream wafer. The Walls ice cream man was a familiar sight in the 1920s and 1930s, with his peaked cap and blue jacket, riding his tricycle with an ice box of ice cream and snow fruits (the forerunner of the ice lolly) in front of him. In bold white lettering on a blue background was the slogan, "Stop Me and Buy One".

Jimmy Rochford was an amusing character, a soap box orator who entertained crowds at Alexandra Park gates. One night he would give the Conservative Party a real drubbing, while boosting the merits of the Labour Party. Then a couple of nights later the order would be reversed; the Tory Party was great and the Labour Party was a load of rubbish. His "speechifying" was always lighthearted, interspersed with topical humour and accompanied by much gesticulation. I think the subject of his speech was often chosen to fit in with his jokes, rather than the other way about.

The two largest dance halls in this part of Manchester at the time were the Embassy Ballroom, Withington Road, facing Yarburgh Street, and the Chorlton Palais on Barlow Moor Road. There were several large public, private, parish and Co-operative halls where dances and other functions were regularly held. Today almost every place of entertainment has a bar and drinking licence, but dance halls then did not have such amenities. Despite the fact that "pass-outs" were "men only" and girls who left the room were not allowed back, I don't remember anybody making noises about sex discrimination. Some places even charged two or three pence for a "pass-out". Most dance halls had an interval of a quarter hour, so if the nearest pub was five minutes' sprint away, the band lads only had five minutes to quench their thirsts – not much, especially for a wind instrument player. The problem was often solved by meeting early at some pub to have a couple of pints before making their way to the dance hall. Many of the musicians put a large bottle of their favourite brew in their instrument case, to be enjoyed backstage.

I cannot leave the area without mentioning the largest landmark – Manchester City Football Ground – and the many fine players who displayed their skills there during the period between the wars. Manchester

City moved from their compact ground at Bennett Street to the expanse of the Maine Road ground in 1923. The terraces were then only covered on one side, above the dressing rooms, for seated spectators, but the ground accommodated more spectators than any other club ground in England - more than 84,000 on one occasion. The legendary Billy Meredith played his last game there in a cup-tie in his fiftieth year. At that time there was another Welsh Wizard who played on the opposite wing to Meredith in the Welsh international team, Ted Vizard, who played for Bolton Wanderers in the first Wembley cup final in 1923.

Some other great footballers I had the pleasure of seeing grace the turf of the Maine Road ground with their artistry were big Frank Swift, goalkeeper superb, the ex Fleetwood and Blackpool fisherman and boatman; the strong, forceful international left winger, Eric Brook (Brookie); Horace Barnes, with his terrific left foot shot; Georgie Hicks, a local lad who made good, and Sammy Cowan, probably the most underrated centre half this century. Other great footballers I saw at Maine Road include super goal-getter Dixie Dean of Everton; his great rival goalscorer, George Camsell of Middlesbrough; Hooper and Rimmell, goal scoring wingers of Sheffield Wednesday, and the never to be forgotten Stanley Matthews of Stoke City and Blackpool, whose dazzling footwork was, to put it mildly, magic and baffling.

Making the new Manchester City ground, 1922

The Wireless

In the summer of 1922, interest was being displayed in reports of broadcasting in America, and from June onwards the original 2LO London station of the Marconi Company - then experimental - received temporary licences for broadcasting occasional concerts for charitable purposes.

There was soon a popular demand for regular broadcasting, and when several manufacturers of radio apparatus applied for licences to transmit, it was decided that a single broadcasting company should be formed. The result was the British Broadcasting Company, which undertook to erect eight stations of 3 kilowatts input and to transmit from them a daily programme "to the reasonable satisfaction of the Post Master General".

The receiving licence sold to the public gave a right to use only a BBC set - one made by a manufacturing member of the Company. On this basis regular broadcasting commenced from London, Birmingham and Manchester. In 1923 many changes were made. A 15/- constructor's licence allowed anyone to make a set of British parts only, and this started off a craze of amateur wireless set construction in the vicinity of the three broadcasting stations, which spread throughout the country as more and more powerful transmitters were erected.

I was a schoolboy at the time, but I well remember the excitement of "helping" my dad make a small crystal set. He bought the parts in town and when I first saw them I couldn't believe it would be possible to reproduce sound from them. Tuning coils had to be wound with the specified length of copper wire; a detector with a crystal and terminals for the attachment of the aerial and earth wires were fixed on to a base board measuring nine inches square. Then, when terminals for headphones had been fixed, the circuit had to be wired up. A length of special wire for earthing the set joined the earth terminal to the cold water

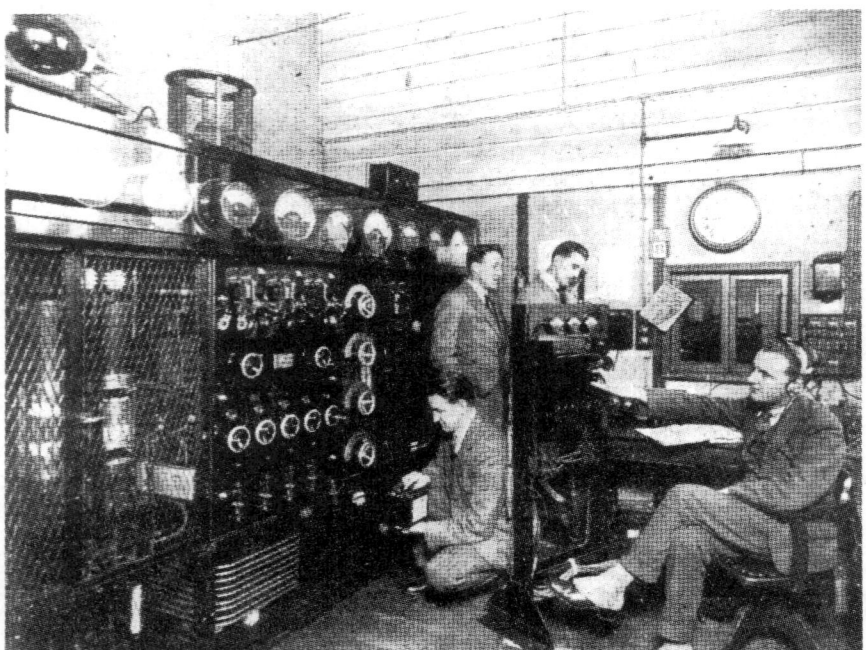

Station 2ZY

tap in the kitchen, the aerial wire was slung across the back bedroom and we were ready to tune in, so I thought. Then Dad broke the sad news; we hadn't got any headphones and he couldn't afford to buy any until the following week. "Ne'er mind, Dad," I said. "It'll be something to look forward to."

Brown's Featherweight Headphones (21/- - nearly half Dad's wages) were considered to be the best on the market. Fortunately he had a three nights engagement at one of the local working men's clubs the following week, so the big thrill was assured, if everything had been wired up correctly.

A week in childhood seems a long time. The days dragged by, but patience was rewarded when Dad brought home the precious Brown's Featherweights on the Saturday afternoon. They were soon connected to the crystal set and operations commenced, twisting the tuning coils and fiddling about with the cat's whisker to find the right spot on the crystal, but without success. Dad had the headphones and, as happens with most fathers with a new toy, he had taken over all operations. After ten minutes his face took on a puzzled look. I was getting impatient. "Let me have a go," I asked several times. In exasperation he handed over the headphones. As I put them on, Dad tightened one of the terminals and to my amazement the sound of music fell upon my ears; the miracle had happened. I shouted, "I can hear it! I can hear music!" It was a wonderful experience, one that anybody under the age of sixty cannot possibly imagine if they have been brought up with a radio in the house.

Our little crystal set was only capable of receiving broadcasts from the 2ZY Manchester station in the old Westinghouse studio in Trafford Park, and music programmes were mostly provided by local artists and musicians. Being interested in dance music, I particularly remember listening to two of the leading semi-professional dance bands, the Garner Schofield Orchestra and the Amazon Six. I was baffled why the band was called the Amazons; it wasn't an all-ladies' orchestra, as I expected, and I am no wiser today.

At a later date, dance music from London was relayed through the Manchester transmitter, and this further stimulated my enthusiasm for jazz and dance music. Such famous bands as the Savoy Orpheans, Havana or Tango Bands, broadcasting live from the Savoy

1922 advertisement

Hotel, or the Hotel Cecil Band could be heard six nights a week between 10.30pm and midnight. Many times I fell asleep listening to the music, to wake up in the early hours of the morning still wearing headphones.

When the old crystal set began to deteriorate it was time we went in for a valve set, so with the aid of a "blue print" issued by the new periodical, Amateur Wireless, a more powerful set was built. Of course, this was more costly to make and operate, needing a loudspeaker and batteries recharging regularly. That chore was finally banished about 1930, when my young brother constructed a four-valve mains receiver, the "Telson 4", with an extension speaker upstairs. Thinking back, I wonder why we had a copper wire connected to the wire coil spring mattress and no outside aerial? Maybe my parents thought that the 10/- a year licence fee did not represent value for money for them, which I can well understand. Mother went out to work at 8.00am, Monday to Saturday,

and rarely got home before ten o'clock at night, while Dad, after coming home at tea-time, was out fulfilling his engagements most nights after tea.

The 1930s and 1940s was probably the "golden age" of radio. It was also the "golden age" of jazz, swing and dance music. The BBC had its own resident band, the Jack Payne Orchestra, which was replaced by the Henry Hall BBC Dance Orchestra, specially formed for the purpose of broadcasting. There were some superb bands on the air, each with its own style, vocalists and signature tune. I used to look forward to the late night dance music, from 10.30pm to midnight every night except Sunday, when such fine bands as those of Roy Fox, Lew Stone, Bert Ambrose, Jack Hylton, Billy Cotton, Harry Roy, Sidney Lipton, Edmundo Ross and Maurice Winnick (a Manchester man) made regular broadcasts.

The year 1933 was for me the highlight of pre-war dance band broadcasting when I heard the magnificent sound of

My Manchester

the Duke Ellington Orchestra for the first time in my life. My immediate reaction was to buy the records of such numbers as "Solitude", "Mood Indigo", "Creole Love Call" and "Merry go Round" and these 78 rpm records remain in my possession to this day.

During the 1930s the BBC broadcast many variety shows, singers, bands, solo instrumentalists and comedians: such splendid double acts as Layton and Johnstone, Western Brothers, Bennett and Williams and the two Leslies singing their own and the popular songs of the day. There was always a good laugh to be had from comedians such as Rob Wilton; Will Hay, with his schoolmaster sketches; Stainless Stephen, the Sheffield comedian with his punctuated humour; the great Rochdale dame, Norman Evans; the cockney Cheekie Chappie, Max Miller, and the hilarious Arthur Askey. In those days the variety artists fitted their wireless broadcasts in between their tours and theatre engagements.

Next to the King's Christmas Day speech to the nation, for volume of listeners, came the English Cup Final from Wembley, when, as play progressed, one commentator could be heard interrupting with the simple comment of, "Square two", pause, "Square four", pause, "Square seven", pause, "Square eight". The Radio Times printed a diagram of the football field, divided into eight squares so that listeners could follow the movement of play. Next, I think, came the Varsity Boat Race on the Thames, with John Snagge's familiar, "In-out in-out", followed by the Grand National and the Derby.

The importance of commercial radio must be mentioned here. British broadcasting was divided into regions and there was no advertising. However, British firms advertised their goods regularly from transmitters on the other side of the English Channel, mainly Radio Luxemburg, a favourite station with millions of British listeners, particularly on Sundays or in the early hours of the morning when British stations had closed down. Ovaltine certainly impressed their name on the public via Radio Luxemburg, with their "Little Ovaltinies" song and programme advertising. I remember a popular "closing down" tune used by Radio Normandy, which became a favourite "last waltz" number for many of the local dance halls and dance bands.

The period between the two Great Wars was probably the glorious age of the cinema, when most people went to the pictures at least once a week. The Manchester area had an abundance of cinemas, the best and biggest being in the city centre and residential suburbs. New films were first shown at the city centre picture houses, where seats were dearer, before going to the posher suburbs, so it could be weeks, or even months, before a film was featured at the cinemas in the poorer districts such as Ancoats, Beswick, Hulme, Ardwick, Chorlton-on-Medlock, Bradford, Lower Openshaw, Strangeways, Cheetham or Collyhurst. The picture houses in those areas, frequently referred to as "flea pits" or "bug huts", generally had poor seating, sometimes bare wooden forms, but who cared? You could always sit on your jacket or cap, and it only cost a penny at the Saturday afternoon matinee and two or three pence at the twice-nightly performances.

Most city cinemas were on Peter Street, Oxford Street and Oxford Road. Starting from Deansgate, first came the Futurist, followed by the Tivoli, Gaiety and Theatre Royal on Peter Street; then came the Paramount and New Oxford on Oxford Street. The Tatler, showing newsreels and cartoons, was at the bottom of Oxford Road Station approach. Next came the Regal, opposite Charles Street, and on the corner of Grosvenor Street,

The author in 1933

October 1935